PRAISE FOR
WORKING CONJURE

"Sen Moise teaches the traditions of his ancestors and kindly shares their wisdom with us. Rooted in the past, he speaks eloquently on why these things apply to us today in the modern world without compromise."

—CHRISTOPHER PENCZAK, cofounder of the
Temple of Witchcraft

"Written with a heaping helping of Southern grace and charm, and sweetened with a dash of humor, Working Conjure is akin to sitting down to coffee and beignets with a treasured friend: a rich and delectable treat, coupled with delightful conversation and newfound strength and vigor. What Hoodoo Sen Moise serves up between these pages is nothing short of amazing. It's the most satisfying book you'll ever read—and it will change your life forever!"

—DOROTHY MORRISON, author of *Everyday
Magic* and *Utterly Wicked*

"Hoodoo Sen Moise has devoted a lifetime to becoming one of the best of the best in Conjure. In Working Conjure, his beautifully written and engaging book, Sen Moise shares his phenomenal knowledge, wisdom, and advice, making the fundamentals of Conjure accessible to everyone. What's more, this is a deeply spiritual book that will connect you to your roots, both on Earth and in spirit."

—ROSEMARY ELLEN GUILEY, author of
Guide to Psychic Protection

"Working Conjure *is a blessing. With the increasing commodification of African American and African Diasporic traditions, books about our practices that are simple, direct, and useful seem few and far between. Hoodoo Sen Moise manages to balance a solid delivery on the practice of Conjure with just enough theory to create a foundation to do this spiritual work—which is not, as he also reminds us, 'spiritual easy'—and to continue the work given to us by our ancestors to heal each other and the world we share."*

—MAMBO CHITA TANN, author of *Haitian Vodou*

"We're very blessed to have such great knowledge of the traditional way of doing Hoodoo Conjure, as you'll find in Working Conjure, *an understanding workbook of the Hoodoo Conjure tradition that also teaches it's true history. All who read it are truly blessed with great knowledge. I highly recommend* Working Conjure *to anyone who is starting out or is already an advanced worker. Be blessed."*

—PAYSHENCE SMITH, of the Rev. Payshence
Spiritual Ministry

"Working Conjure *is a must have on the bookshelf of anyone interested in Southern folk magic. Hoodoo Sen Moise brings us the time-worn teachings that have evolved in the southern United States over hundreds of years. This practical book teaches you how you can use Conjure in everyday situations and discover the power and perseverance of the Southern spirit to evolve, change, transform, manifest, and heal. Hoodoo Sen Moise has presented a great work for these traditions, weaving together magic and spiritual belief!"*

—BRIAN CAIN, Alexandrian high priest and cohost
of HexFest and Festival of the Dead

"Working Conjure *is the folk magic book we've all been waiting for! Packed with expert knowledge, detailed instructions, accurate history, and never-before-revealed secrets for powerful Conjure, this is a must-have in your magical library for its accuracy and authenticity that only one born into a Conjure family can provide. A superb book on Hoodoo, Conjure, and folk magic for both the beginning or experienced practitioner, written by the highly experienced and renowned Hoodoo, Vodou and Conjure Man of New Orleans himself!"*

—ANNA E. PARMELEE, founder and owner of
Erzulie's Voodoo store, New Orleans

"Working Conjure *is a beautifully written book with loads of valuable information on the traditions of African-American Conjure and Hoodoo. This book will enlighten a seasoned conjurer and give a sound foundation to a new practitioner of Conjure and set them on the right path. Hoodoo Sen Moise put his heart and soul into the writing of this book and it comes across on every page."*

—LELIA MARINO of Ms. Rain's Conjure Shop

"*I was excited to read Sen Moise's new book* Working Conjure. *The book is clear, direct, and much needed in the world of Hoodoo and Conjure. Sen Moise tells it like it is and brings good insight and history into the hows and whys of the tradition, putting to rest a lot of inaccuracies floating around in these days of internet experts. Now there is a book that speaks clearly to those wishing to know more about authentic Hoodoo and Conjure."*

—CANDELO KIMBISA, Spiritualist radio personality
and host of *Candelo's Corner,* America's longest
running Palo Mayombé talk show.

Working Conjure

A Guide to Hoodoo Folk Magic

HOODOO SEN MOISE

WEISER BOOKS

This edition first published in 2018 by Weiser Books, an imprint of
Red Wheel/Weiser, LLC

With offices at:
65 Parker Street, Suite 7
Newburyport, MA 01950
www.redwheelweiser.com

All Bible passages are taken from the King James version.

ISBN: 978-1-57863-627-3

Library of Congress Cataloging-in-Publication Data available upon request.

Cover design by Kathryn Sky-Peck
Cover art © Robert Cronk III
Interior by Maureen Forys, Happenstance Type-O-Rama
Typeset in Adobe Caslon Pro and Caslon Antique

Printed in Canada

MAR

10 9 8 7 6 5

This book is dedicated to the Ancestors and the sacrifices they made so that we all
can be standing where we are right now. The love, wisdom, and guidance of those
who came before me give everything and for that I am truly grateful.

CONTENTS

INTRODUCTION

A Day in the Life of a Conjure Man

On a cool autumn day in Georgia, the leaves of the trees were turning from green to orange and gold, while some were transitioning to brown. Both the trees and the surrounding area were truly beautiful to behold. A nice breeze shuffled the leaves that had already fallen.

As evening approached, the sun began to work its way down to allow for night to begin. The potent transformation of light to dark was starting—the time when spirits are awakening. The day is for the living and the night is for the dead, you see. After the sun was gone, a man dressed in dark-colored pants and a red shirt approached the graveyard next to one of the local churches. This man had a cigar in his left hand, a bottle of whiskey in his right, and his head was covered with a navy blue cloth. This was a Conjure man or Hoodoo man. Conjure and Hoodoo are terms that have become synonymous with one another and can be used interchangeably.

He walked up to the entrance of the graveyard and acknowledged the gates. The man reached into his pocket and pulled out a few coins. Holding the coins in his hand, he displayed them to the directions—East, West, North, and South—made a small prayer, and then dropped them at the graveyard gates. Holding his lit cigar and his bottle of whiskey, he entered and made his way to the crossroads within the graveyard. Once there, he began his work.

The man pulled a trowel out of his back pocket and dug a small hole at the crossroads. The ground was a little firm, so the digging process was labored. The hole was about ten inches deep and about eight inches around. After ten minutes of digging, the hole was complete.

The man gave thanks to the ancestors and to the earth for taking on the work that was being performed. He took a few more coins (a quarter, a dime, a nickel, and a penny), once again oriented them to the four directions, and tossed them into the hole. He then poured whiskey on top of the coins at the bottom of the opened earth, making offerings to the spirits in the graveyard, as well as the earth for the work.

Once the offerings were placed into the ground, the man pulled a brown paper bag out of his back pocket. Several items were in this bag.

A photograph of a young man was wrapped in twine that had been soaked in a special oil known as Separation Oil. The man had also put Hot Foot Powder (you'll find the formula on page 171) in the bag, as well as a few other roots and charms.

The bag with everything in it was placed into the hole. He called out to some of the spirits of the graveyard with whom he had established a relationship, asking them to bring separation to the young man in the photo. The Conjure man asked that the man in the photo be separated from the relationship he was in and that he be moved away. Once his prayers and declarations were complete, the Conjure man covered the hole and, once again, poured whiskey over the top.

The man got up and put the trowel back in his pocket. He then gave thanks to the spirits of the graveyard who had come to his assistance and heard his declarations. He walked back to the gates of the graveyard, thanked the spirits of the gates, and made his way back home.

Earlier that day, this man had received a visit from a young woman, someone who had been coming to him for quite some time. She had expressed her fears and overwhelming sadness regarding her relationship with her boyfriend. She described her boyfriend as abusive, controlling, and a raging alcoholic. She said how fearful she was of him, as he would say things like she "wasn't going anywhere," or that he would make sure she was unable to leave. The woman was crying and confused.

The Conjure man offered his counsel and the two spoke for a good while. The young woman knew that he was a rootworker, someone who could work the elements of magic to create a change in her present situation and so she asked for his help in removing the abusive boyfriend from her life.

The Condition of Conjure

In the realm of spiritual or magic work, Hoodoo or Conjure has a tremendous influence in creating change that may not be so likely to occur otherwise. This is due, in part, to the nature of Conjure. Conjure was birthed out of a need to stop oppression and as a way to gain a leg up on the slave masters so that folks could be free from the constant and disgusting treatment they received at the hand of those who took them away from everything they knew and loved. The power of the *roots*, coupled with the spirits of the ancestors, forms a bond that facilitates magical change. When I say roots, I am referring to every part of the plant. That includes the root, the leaf, the stem, the flowers, and even the seeds. The term *root* is used as an umbrella term for all of these things in the parlance of Conjure.

The work just described shows a day in the life of a Conjure man. The story is filled with actions that folks may or may not be familiar with. Now, I would like to explain the steps in the story to help you understand how this powerful practice and work can be achieved.

We began with the Conjure man coming to the graveyard at the point of dusk. Why dusk? There is an old saying that the day is for the living and the night is for the dead. The reason for this is because there are points of transition that are inclusive of both seen and unseen (the spirits themselves). It is like a veil worn by a bride. Her face is at least somewhat masked, until it is time for her to be revealed. Spirits are not that far removed from this principle. As living beings, our bodies have internal clocks. The majority of the time, the clock is in sync with the day and the night. During the day, we are awake, alert, and doing whatever tasks need to be done. When night comes, we get tired and our physical bodies begin to call for rest. We have transitioned from the work time to the time of being in a cocoon. That cocoon is sleep, rest, and recharging for the next day. For most living folks, our proverbial veils are put on at night and taken off during the day. Of course we know that there are some individuals who are nocturnal and function better at night than they do in the day. As humans, we are incredibly diverse. However, this is how the general principle of the living and the dead works, as I was given it.

Spirits (the dead), on the other hand, have the opposite process of this veil. They, for the most part, are veiled in the day and unveiled at night. A significant reason for this is because they are not housed within a body and their time of awakening is the opposite of our own. It is important to note that the physical and spirit worlds are two reflective mirrors that parallel one another, but in an opposite manner. As we sleep, they tend to rise. As we work, they tend to rest.

Once the Conjure man arrived at the gates of the graveyard, he gave offerings at the entrance. It is like knocking on the door of someone's house. Offerings are quite important because they are conduits of balance. If something is given, then something is taken. If something is taken then something is given. You see, he was going into the graveyard to do spiritual work with the dead and you have to pay for the work you are doing. The offerings given have a couple of purposes. The first is to pay for work that is being done and the second is to *elevate* as well as motivate the spirits you are working with. By elevate I mean to lift up—to speak prayers, give words of thanksgiving, make offerings, and the like.

Upon entering the graveyard, the Conjure man began to give thanks to those that came before him. He acknowledged the sacrifices that were made so that he could be standing exactly where he was at the time he was. He gave thanks to the earth, which possesses an astronomical amount of magical power to transform and create change that reflects into both the world of the spirit and the world of the physical. Giving thanks is a form of elevation and of calling out to the spirits so that we can gain their attention and receive their help. Once he began to dig the hole, he was creating a womb, so to speak, in which the work could be birthed.

Soil, or dirt, possesses power, energies, and spirits that are both creative and destructive. Where the soil comes from indicates what it will do. We will discuss this in further detail in chapter 5, but just know that the *dirts* themselves are potent magical ingredients that birth work from the spiritual into the physical.

When the Conjure man finished digging the hole, he had with him a bag with several items in it—items that were very personal to a particular individual. You see, one of the foundation stones of Conjure is that of linking the work to an individual (or individuals) and linking the individual to the work. This is accomplished by way of items that hold a piece of that individual. A photograph, hair, fingernails, and so forth, all carry a link, an essence of a person, and are used to attach the work to them, whatever work that may be. The terms *personal concerns, links,* or sometimes, *tokens,* are used to describe such items, depending on where you come from.

In his work, the man was executing in the physical what he wanted to manifest into the spiritual. As I was explaining earlier about the two mirrors, when something is done in the physical, it will reflect into the spiritual and vice versa. The work is about getting the two to match and reflect, which is a major part of what we do in Conjure.

- The Conjure man "tied up" the individual in the photo, so that he would be prevented (bound) from doing anything against the Conjure man's client.

- Separation Oil was put on the string used to bind the photograph to keep him away from her.

- Hot Foot Powder was added to the work to make him physically move out of the picture.

- The Conjure man then buried the bag containing the work at the crossroads of the graveyard, so that every road or opportunity would be shut down with the assistance of all the spirits that resided there.

Once his work was complete, the Conjure Man gave thanks (again elevating the spirits of the graveyard) and left the work in the womb of the earth to be birthed so that the change and desired goal could and would be achieved.

In this book, we will discuss principles of Conjure in magic today. You will learn the fundamentals of Conjure practice that will set the stage for building relationships with the spirits of the roots and the magic they hold. Conjure has very strong roots in the earth and the spirits of the earth, which is important in balancing the physical with the spiritual and because if you have no foundation, there is nothing to set one's magical work upon to manifest between those two realms.

The book contains recipes and workings that allow you to begin this journey, experience the culture, and see the latent power that is embodied in this potent magical practice. The knowledge of how to work a root is one that every Conjure man or woman must possess. It comes from understanding the spirits of the roots, the ancestors, and the foundation of the two worlds that reflect into one another.

In today's world, we come across all sorts of folks who practice all sorts of things and have many different perspectives. This book reflects my own perspectives as a Conjure man.

ooooo

For the past 35 years, my life has been dedicated to the spirits, to the roots, and to the work. It is the work that sustains us. It is the work that opens doors and closes them. It is the work that provokes growth. That's what Conjure is about, after all. I will show you the balance of working with both hands—metaphors for positive and negative magical working, why it is necessary, and how the less-spoken-about facets of the work are just as important as those that are talked about more openly. The ways that you can work to create change are vital in this very magical practice. We will go over ways to work with both hands that give you tools to use in your own daily life. Nature itself is the shining example of both sides of the coin. A rainstorm can give needed water to the plants as well as create a destructive flood. Just as life has all sorts of ups and downs, our work can be used to take on those challenges effectively.

Balance has always been a cornerstone of the practice of Conjure. Whether it is to bless or heal, to trick or damn, the balance of both hands is represented in order to have an approach that keeps the scales in line.

Change can be good, bad, or neutral. That change, whichever facet of it, should always bring about the opportunity for growth as well as a sharpening of your work. So, let's grow, let's learn, and let's see about that Conjure life!

1

WHAT IS CONJURE/ HOODOO?

In many places in America, particularly the South, you will hear terms such as *Hoodoo, Conjure, rootwork,* or *work* used to describe a magical practice that is intended to bring about change in one way or another. These terms have become synonymous with one another and are used to describe the same thing. From here on out, we will use the word Conjure to refer to this magical practice.

So then, what is Conjure? The short answer would be that Conjure is an African American-based magical practice that contains influences from African spiritual practices, Christianity, Jewish mysticism, and Native American practices, as well as European folk magic. However, the primary influence derives from the spiritual beliefs of Central and West Africa.

During the transatlantic slave trades, many Africans were forced from their homes, their families, their spirituality, and all they had known, and taken to the Caribbean, and then to the Americas. These slaves hailed primarily from the western and central regions—places such as the Congo, Benin, and Nigeria. Their varying religious and spiritual beliefs became a great influence in the Caribbean and the Americas.[1] In the United States, the atrocity of the slave trade offically continued until 1808, when importation of slaves from Africa was outlawed. Of course, this is not to say that the smuggling of slaves did not occur afterward.

The Church, both Catholic and Protestant denominations, saw African religions, spiritualities, and belief systems as evil, immoral, and even murderous. It was assumed that things like devil worship, human sacrifice, and a variety of other unethical acts were a part of their practices and so, these magnificent people, the enslaved Africans, were prevented from honoring their spirits and worshiping in the ways of their culture. Instead, Christianity was forced upon them in order to encourage or increase the slave master's control. You see, if they worshipped the god of the slave master, then the slave master would have tighter reins and, thus, there would be fewer attempts at flight or revolt.

Under these circumstances, you might see how this sad state of affairs would create feelings of despair and hopelessness. However, some of the enslaved did find ways to overcome. Some continued their practices in secret, which was dangerous, as, if caught, repercussions included beatings, whippings, murder, rape, physical harm to loved ones who were also slaves, as well as taking away the little food they were given. It was primarily the fear of those repercussions that kept them from rebelling against their horrible circumstances.

Others, however, were more innovative—they encouraged slave masters to believe they were worshiping the Christian way when in reality they were just using it as a mask to continue, as best they could, the practices of their own people. They would hold fast the spiritual beliefs of their culture and overcome the

---

[1] Long, Caroline Morrow, "Spiritual Merchants: Religion, Magic and Commerce" from the chapter "African Origins and European Influences."

oppression that continually dealt an almost unbearable burden. It is from this that we find Christianity making its way into the practice we know today as Conjure.

Conjure was born in the United States out of the absolute need to overcome oppression, to create opportunity, and to provide the ability to magically stick up the middle finger to their oppressors. It was a way to counter the deeds of the slave masters and execute works of rebellion against those who would enslave and commit atrocities against them. This work was desperately needed, and it was the spirits of these slaves and their ancestors that evolved into Conjure—one of the most potent spiritual and magical practices.

ooooo

The working side of Conjure was greatly influenced by the religious beliefs of the Congo region. They were one of its primary roots. The idea that spirits reside in the trees, the leaves, the roots, and the earth, and that they hold power to facilitate change became an important staple in the fabric of what we know as Conjure today.

The meaning of *change*, as used here, is an appearance of one realm or world into the other. We do work to create a new reality. The reality that you need a job or healing, for example, is apparent in the physical but perhaps not yet seen in the spirit. The spirits of the roots work between both worlds so the reflection is seen on both sides. In this case, the healing you are looking for or the job you need is not only open to you, but also the fruit of the work you have done to acquire these things is made known in this world by the physical evidence. When the spirit and physical worlds are mirroring one another, you get the job and the sickness you had is no longer plaguing you. Simply put, it is the outward manifestation of the inner work as well as the inner manifestation of the outward work. The balance of both sides, both worlds, and both realities.

The altering of reality is effected by means of doing work with these spirits or essences that assist you in reaching the desired goal. It is using these natural and primal powers of the roots that were given to us by God that allows for our own edification, forward movement, and evolution to make our daily lives better.

The power of the root is one of primal beginnings. The spirits of the roots provide a touch of the divine, and these spirits work in conjunction with us to make things happen that will, ultimately, create change in one way or another. For example, let's say that everywhere you turn the roads seem blocked, like nothing is, in the language of Conjure, "opened up for you." It could be that the *crossroads,* the place of opportunity and open doors, is closed to you.

Why the crossroads? Well, the crossroads is a place of power, where the realm of the physical meets the realm of the spirit. It is the place where our paths are laid before us and, if it has been closed to us, we will absolutely see blockages all around. So, you would want to take some offerings to the crossroads and do a work to open it up.

You might take a coconut, place some of your hair, fingernail, or toenail clippings, together with a photo, some red palm oil, and some sugar inside, and take it to the crossroads. There you might give the crossroads offerings of whiskey or rum as well as smoke while you ask the spirits who reside there—and there are many—to open the way. All the while you are digging a hole in which to bury your work. Once that has been done, the crossroads, your paths, will open up for you again. This is just one of many works that can be done for a circumstance such as this, but the point I am making here is that these roots, dirts, leaves, and such hold power to create manifestations in both the spirit and the physical realms. This fundamental tenet is one we rootworkers hold to in order to effectively work Conjure.

Influences in Conjure

Conjure varies from region to region, as well as from family to family. Why is that? Well, to put it simply, some regions had more of one influence than another. Other regions had certain roots that were more easily accessible. You also have the influence of the families that lived in those regions whose own folk practices became incorporated into Conjure.

In the South, you will find folks who sweep their houses from back to front, not only to clean the floor, but also to begin a cleansing on their home. You will find others will put a railroad spike in the corner of their property to protect it. The reason for the spike is because it *nails down* or fortifies your home, preventing negativity or evil from being able to enter the property.

When I was a kid, we used to keep a glass of water, with evil eye beads inside, by the door. Once a week, a candle would be lit and set next to the glass, as it was believed that the evil eye could not survive under the water. If someone was trying to give you the evil eye, the glass by the door would take the hit. You see, these magical practices are very much intertwined in the stories that have been passed down by families and have become a big part of the Conjure works you see today.

Conjure is not a religion or spiritual path, per se, but rather magic/spiritual work that is done to bring about change in a situation. Whether that situation is a relationship, money, a job, revenge, healing, or cleansing, the fundamental tenet of Conjure is to do work that changes the circumstance.

Now, the work of Conjure can be, and is in some areas, largely used in conjunction with regional spiritual practices. In

New Orleans, for example, the population of the city is largely Roman Catholic. The Catholic church makes up a large part of the city's spiritual beliefs. Many rootworkers are in attendance at the weekly masses. Likewise, you will find that the working of Conjure in conjunction with the Catholic saints is very common in New Orleans. Take St. Expedite, also known as Saint Expeditus, for example. In life, Expedite was a Roman soldier who, it is said, converted to Christianity and was beheaded in 303 C.E. He had a reputation for getting things accomplished with haste. Because of this he is typically a saint that folks go to when they need fast results due to time constraints or other urgencies. He is greatly loved and worked with, both inside and outside of the Catholic faith. Catholic rootworkers will go to him, give offerings, and leave work so that things happen swiftly and the favors are answered quickly.

Usually, with St. Expedite, you make a deal with him. The deal is that you will give him offerings once he grants the petition you make. So, for example, if you are looking to get some money in a hurry to pay bills, you would make your prayers to him and tell him that if he grants the petition in a hurry, you will give him offerings, such as pound cake, water, candles (red, white, or yellow), and flowers. Now, it is very important that you honor that promise. When you tell a spirit, saint, or whomever that you are going to do something, you need to do it. Remember, if they grant something for you they can easily take it away. And they would be completely justified in doing so because you didn't hold up your end of the bargain.

A few years ago, I was looking around in a Catholic church in New Orleans. I saw the beautiful statues, stained glass, and altar pieces and was in awe of how the place looked. I happened to come upon the area where prayer candles could be lit for people. It was a touching sight, for sure. There were all these candles lit for various prayers and petitions, all seated in a beautiful stand.

While I was admiring the stand and the lights that had been set, I noticed something underneath the candle stand, behind one of the iron legs. It was a mojo hand—a little charm bag—that had a St. Expedite prayer card wrapped around it. It had been placed under all of the lights that had been set in the church for whatever work the Conjure person was doing. I did not, of course, touch the work being done. That would just be rude. I did, however, greatly respect the work that was being done with the two paths together. It was Conjure and Catholicism working in conjunction with one another—faith and work coming together to achieve the desired goal. The power of the roots working in tandem with the power of the saint. It was a beautiful example of how the inner work of faith moves with the outer work of Conjure.

ooooo

In areas where Protestant Christianity is dominant, you will find its signature on the rootworker's work as well. Remember, Conjure in and of itself is a powerful relationship with the root that is used in tandem with the faiths or spiritual paths that have influenced and expanded upon it by combining inner faith with outer work. The Old Testament, for example, is very widely used in working Conjure.

Whether or not this pleases people, there is a profound Christian influence on Conjure. Genesis, Psalms, Proverbs, and other books of the Bible, for example, hold keys of power in them. The keys of power in these books are made up of several things. There are *spells* or *workings*—spiritual principles of power to create magical change and potent spiritual work that will manifest in a physical way—actually contained in the Bible that we use quite frequently.

When I say *books* of the Bible, I am referring to just that. For example, Genesis, Psalms, Proverbs, and Isaiah are all smaller books that make up the larger book. Now, is it only Christian influence that is the foundation of what we know as Conjure today? Absolutely not. The African root of Conjure is still the primary root.

The influences of the Kongo, Yoruba, and Fon people dominate how work is done within the realm of this potent practice. The African spiritual practices that were, and still are, nature and ancestral based hold extreme significance in the power of the work.

Let's take, for example, the *doll baby*, also known as a dollie or Voodoo doll. The doll is made from items typically available in the rootworker's region. Dolls might be made from sticks and Spanish moss with a fabric wrapped around them to form the body. They can also be made with twine and cotton. There are many ways to create a doll baby that have been and are still being used to this day.

One of the purposes of the doll baby is to do work on an individual, whether positive or negative, by way of a link established through an individual's personal items: hair, blood, fingernail clippings, and the like. A doll baby may also be used to house a spirit that work is done with, often on a contractual basis, as a way of having the spirit work through the vessel of the doll.

In the Congo, there are large wooden statues called *Nkisi*. These statues typically have a hollowed-out area, usually in the stomach or behind the head, in which special roots, bones, and powders are placed for the working spirit that will inhabit it. Nails are then driven into it to activate the statue—or large wooden doll, if you will. The purpose of driving the nails into the Nkisi is to wake up the inhabiting spirit and give them an assignment to carry out. Here, we find a strong commonality with the American version of the Voodoo doll, and we can also see parallels between the nails hammered into the Nkisi and the pins stuck in the doll.

When enslaved Kongolese were transported to the Americas, they could not make Nkisi statues for several reasons. First of all, they lacked the materials needed to carve them. Second, the appearance and massive size of the statues made them extremely visible, which would have brought about some of those horrible repercussions mentioned earlier. An alternative was needed. And so, here comes a doll that is smaller, easier to hide, and yet still effective.

So as you can see, the spiritual influences of several cultures have played a part in the evolution of Conjure today. It is a practice that has its hands in many houses, so to speak.

A Rootworker's Explanation of Conjure

When we think about Conjure, several things come to mind. Terms such as "putting a root" on someone or "laying a trick" often follow in those thoughts. These terms are fantastic to explain the very practical side and nature of Conjure work.

Conjure is a relationship established with the roots, through which work can be effectively accomplished. A relationship with the root? Yes. You see, a tenet of rootwork is that God has put every plant and animal on Earth for the use and benefit of humanity—and not only for food purposes, but also for magical work. Each root possesses a spirit that holds a connection to the earth and has a predisposition to do certain kinds of work.

Here are two quotes from the Bible regarding the plants and animals. The first comes from Psalm 104:

104 Bless the Lord, O my soul. O Lord my God, thou art very great; thou art clothed with honour and majesty.

2 Who coverest thyself with light as with a garment: who stretchest out the heavens like a curtain:

3 Who layeth the beams of his chambers in the waters: who maketh the clouds his chariot: who walketh upon the wings of the wind:

4 Who maketh his angels spirits; his ministers a flaming fire:

5 Who laid the foundations of the earth, that it should not be removed for ever.

6 Thou coveredst it with the deep as with a garment: the waters stood above the mountains.

7 At thy rebuke they fled; at the voice of thy thunder they hasted away.

8 They go up by the mountains; they go down by the valleys unto the place which thou hast founded for them.

9 Thou hast set a bound that they may not pass over; that they turn not again to cover the earth.

10 He sendeth the springs into the valleys, which run among the hills.

11 They give drink to every beast of the field: the wild asses quench their thirst.

12 By them shall the fowls of the heaven have their habitation, which sing among the branches.

13 He watereth the hills from his chambers: the earth is satisfied with the fruit of thy works.

14 He causeth the grass to grow for the cattle, and herb for the service of man: that he may bring forth food out of the earth;

15 And wine that maketh glad the heart of man, and oil to make his face to shine, and bread which strengtheneth man's heart.

16 The trees of the Lord are full of sap; the cedars of Lebanon, which he hath planted;

17 Where the birds make their nests: as for the stork, the fir trees are her house.

18 The high hills are a refuge for the wild goats; and the rocks for the conies.

19 He appointed the moon for seasons: the sun knoweth his going down.

20 Thou makest darkness, and it is night: wherein all the beasts of the forest do creep forth.

21 The young lions roar after their prey, and seek their meat from God.

22 The sun ariseth, they gather themselves together, and lay them down in their dens.

23 Man goeth forth unto his work and to his labour until the evening.

24 O Lord, how manifold are thy works! in wisdom hast thou made them all: the earth is full of thy riches.

25 SO IS THIS GREAT AND WIDE SEA, WHEREIN ARE THINGS CREEPING INNUMERABLE, BOTH SMALL AND GREAT BEASTS.

26 THERE GO THE SHIPS: THERE IS THAT LEVIATHAN, WHOM THOU HAST MADE TO PLAY THEREIN.

27 THESE WAIT ALL UPON THEE; THAT THOU MAYEST GIVE THEM THEIR MEAT IN DUE SEASON.

28 THAT THOU GIVEST THEM THEY GATHER: THOU OPENEST THINE HAND, THEY ARE FILLED WITH GOOD.

29 THOU HIDEST THY FACE, THEY ARE TROUBLED: THOU TAKEST AWAY THEIR BREATH, THEY DIE, AND RETURN TO THEIR DUST.

30 THOU SENDEST FORTH THY SPIRIT, THEY ARE CREATED: AND THOU RENEWEST THE FACE OF THE EARTH.

31 THE GLORY OF THE LORD SHALL ENDURE FOR EVER: THE LORD SHALL REJOICE IN HIS WORKS.

32 HE LOOKETH ON THE EARTH, AND IT TREMBLETH: HE TOUCHETH THE HILLS, AND THEY SMOKE.

33 I WILL SING UNTO THE LORD AS LONG AS I LIVE: I WILL SING PRAISE TO MY GOD WHILE I HAVE MY BEING.

34 MY MEDITATION OF HIM SHALL BE SWEET: I WILL BE GLAD IN THE LORD.

35 LET THE SINNERS BE CONSUMED OUT OF THE EARTH, AND LET THE WICKED BE NO MORE. BLESS THOU THE LORD, O MY SOUL. PRAISE YE THE LORD.

The second is from Genesis 1:29–31:

29 AND GOD SAID, BEHOLD, I HAVE GIVEN YOU EVERY HERB BEARING SEED, WHICH IS UPON THE FACE OF ALL THE EARTH, AND EVERY TREE, IN THE WHICH IS THE

FRUIT OF A TREE YIELDING SEED; TO YOU IT SHALL BE FOR MEAT.

30 AND TO EVERY BEAST OF THE EARTH, AND TO EVERY FOWL OF THE AIR, AND TO EVERY THING THAT CREEPETH UPON THE EARTH, WHEREIN THERE IS LIFE, I HAVE GIVEN EVERY GREEN HERB FOR MEAT: AND IT WAS SO.

31 AND GOD SAW EVERY THING THAT HE HAD MADE, AND, BEHOLD, IT WAS VERY GOOD. AND THE EVENING AND THE MORNING WERE THE SIXTH DAY.

For example, let's consider angelica root. Angelica is a very strong root for shielding and protection. It is like the guardian that goes before you and so it is used in quite a bit of protection work as well as in cleansing. The spirit of the angelica root is one whose inclination is to perform the duties of a protector or guardian angel.

When we establish a relationship with these spirits of the roots, we are creating a bond that goes two ways:

- We serve the spirit of the root

- That spirit does work for us

Balance is crucial in rootwork. This balance of things translates into how and why work is done. When you use a root to do work, you need to pay the root for the work.

Nothing in this life is free, including the working of the root. We give the roots prayers, offerings such as rum or whiskey, smoke, songs, money, and light (a lit candle). These things are part of the give and take of the work. If I want to go to a doctor to make myself feel better because I have a stomachache, I would have to pay him for the work of examining and diagnosing my illness. Chances are he isn't going to do it out of the kindness of his heart. This same principle is very much applicable with the working of roots. Those spirits must also be paid. Petitions and offerings must be given so the spirits of the roots will do the work and do it well.

The relationship established with the roots is one that opens the door for powerful work. Just as we have relationships with ancestors, guides, deities, and the like, the same is equally applicable with the roots. This bond is formed in the same or similar way. You speak to the spirit of the root, you honor the spirit of the root, and you offer to the spirit of the root. As you do this, you find the spirit of the root will offer back. The beginning of the working contract starts here.

The culmination of this work is the understanding that cultural influences, slavery, rebelling against oppression, folk magic, and the stories we are told have a huge part to play in the tradition of Conjure and in its magical potency. Merging together the works that have been passed down by those who have come before us and the strong bond with the root will create a worker who is unshakable in his magic and unyielding in his spiritual labors. This is what Conjure is all about. The power of those who came before you and the strength of your bond with the roots will give you the foundation to walk in tremendous authority and strength.

2

PRINCIPLES OF CONJURE

Living the Life of Conjure

There are many folks who have an idea that Conjure is something you do only when you need or want to work magic. I disagree with this. The work of Conjure was birthed out of a need to overcome the oppression of slavery. It was a way for the slaves to turn the tide against the slave masters and take back, at least in some way, what had been taken from them.

Conjure is much more than the magic work that goes into it. It is a culture of magic, a culture of overcoming obstacles, and a culture of ongoing, daily work that keeps the roads we walk on smoothed out. We do things without even thinking about them. If I were sweeping the floor, for example, and I accidentally ran the broom across my feet, I would automatically lift the broom up and spit on it. Why? Running a broom across the feet can take away luck and blessings and, in some ways, can alter the day in a way that might prove to be challenging. Another example would be that every time I go to the graveyard I always drop coins at the gate or entrance. It is not something I even have to think about because I know that when I go to someone's house I never go empty-handed. These are just some simple examples of how we live and how what we do is in both the spirit world and the physical world.

Conjure holds within it a powerful culture where simply allowing detrimental things to happen is not acceptable. It is through that part of the culture that we never allow ourselves to be defeated, nor do we let the opportunity for defeat to even present itself.

Making Magical Change

One of the most potent places in the work of Conjure is the crossroads. The crossroads is the intersection where the world of the spirit and the world of the physical come together. It is in the crossroads that you see into both worlds and it is in the crossroads that powerful work is done. A foundational principle of Conjure is that each merges into the other.

It is like having two mirrors that reflect into one another. The work that is done in the spirit will reflect into the physical and, on the same note, the work done in the physical will reflect into the spirit. The manifestation of each has its own point of power, but understand that what you do in this world will become manifest in the world of the spirit and vice versa. Using physical things, such as roots, to do spiritual work that effects magical change is just that. For example, an uncrossing can be done by making baths that you take for a specific amount of time. The physical act of taking these baths is sent (or reflected) to the spirit, which begins the process of manifestating the uncrossing. The two work together to achieve the change in the condition you are wanting to remove.

It is all about balance. Conjure is not good or evil, it is necessary. We do not see things in such a way that something is one or the other. Circumstances, conditions, and situations are looked at and worked in such a way that a balance of the proverbial scales is maintained. If the work is justified, then it is justified. If not, then there can be spiritual repercussions. You see, if those scales are unbalanced then chaos will come in and take over. Therefore we do what is necessary to keep things in order. This is also why we work with both the Right and Left Hands.

The work of Conjure is not and never has been about staying in the love and light. It is the responsibility of every worker to keep the scales where they need to be and this is done by working with both hands. Sometimes we do things that are not pleasant and not described as "good." That, however, does not negate the fact that it needs to be done. Again, think of how the ancestors had to overcome the conditions and circumstances they were forced to endure. If it were all pleasantries, then they would not have been able to do what they had to so that they could escape the very clutches of evil that they were subjected to.

Spirits

One of the cornerstones of Conjure is the ancestors. It is the ancestors who blazed the trail for each of us to be where we are right now. It was their blood, sweat, and tears that laid the foundation that enables us to do this work and to create magical change to conditions and circumstances. The importance of establishing a relationship with those who came before you is something that opens doors to powerful spiritual work.

Your ancestors carry with them a tremendous amount of wisdom and have the ability to give direction in your work. All of the sacrifices they made laid the way for you to be able to grow, be protected, work effectively, and hold a spiritual foundation that is unshakable by any storm.

Another foundation stone of Conjure is the roots themselves. Every root (by root, I am referring to roots, herbs, barks, and other parts of plants) has within it a spirit. The spirit of the root gives it the power to do certain kinds of spiritual work, depending on the root. Each has its own disposition, if you will. Some are used in works of prosperity, protection, cleansing, and the like. Others are quite effective in works of crossing up, bad luck, damnation, and such. Knowing the roots is a key when it comes to doing this work. In Conjure, we hold to a truth that God put all of the roots here on the earth for our use, both for food and for spiritual work.

Working with spirits, both your ancestors and the spirits of the roots, it is very important that you understand that having respect for them, honoring them, and establishing a relationship with them is what brings about potency in the things you do.

We always give offerings to our ancestors and to the roots. If something is given then something is taken. If something is taken then something is given. This keeps things in balance and should be looked at as paying for the work being done. For example, if you went to get a haircut, you would be expected to give the barber or hairstylist money for the work they did for you. It's only right!

On that same note, our spirits and the spirits of the roots take offerings to do the work that is asked of them. We love them and they love us. We work for them and they work for us. We give them offerings and they give us things like protection, wisdom, insight, and knowledge we would not have otherwise.

Making prayers and petitions is also something that is quite important. If you don't make prayers, how are they going to know what we are asking them to do? If you aren't lifting them up with words of edification, why would they want to work for you? Something as simple as thanking them for everything they have done and everything they continue to do has its own potencies and serves to increase your own power in the work of Conjure as a whole.

Staple Ingredients in Conjure Work

In Conjure, there are items, ingredients, that you must always have around. They are staples in what we do and are used in nearly everything we do.

The candle is always present for a very simple reason. The candle lights the way, or illuminates the path, to what is about to happen. Think of the candle like a lighthouse on a cliff. The lighthouse guides the ships to it. It draws them to itself. This same principle is what the candle does in work—it brings the spirits closer so that work can be done, unless it has been fixed to do a different job. It is also an offering to spirits.

Water is also important in the work of the spirit. It is a means of travel, a conduit of the spirit, and is present to facilitate just that. Water opens the door, so to speak, for spirits to come through so that the job can be done. It is for this reason that having a glass of water where the work is being done is significant.

Another thing you will see is a selection of roots. You will find a lot of things growing around the house and you will also see jars or bags of dried roots. It is from the root that so much of this work comes and it is by the root that we continue to do the jobs at hand. Roots are ingredients in powders, oils, and the like, which create magical change to conditions that need to be removed, imposed, or amplified.

In Conjure work, a very important factor is making sure a link is established with the individual or individuals that the work is being done on or for. The link that is established is done with personal items from the individual, such as hair, fingernails, blood, semen, unwashed clothing, and the like. Those things hold a piece of the essence of someone and, because of that, they can be used as if the person were present in front of you. Photographs and name papers (pieces of paper with the person's full name written on them) can also be used, but they may not be as strong in comparison to actual items from the person.

All in all, this work is very hands on, very practical, and does not shy away from what needs to be accomplished so that the condition is changed. Conjure is about connecting these things together to create that change. The way it is done holds great power and has the ability to facilitate strong spiritual work.

If you are honorable in your work and your relationship with your spirits, then they will honor you back. When I speak of being honorable, I am referring to whatever you are doing, do it with integrity and balance. There must be balance in all things and the only way to keep that balance is to know how to work with both hands.

3

THE FOUNDATION
LAID BEFORE US
(THE ANCESTORS)

Every home needs a foundation to sit on. Without it, the home is shaky at best and will crumble at the slightest adversity. If a storm comes, a home that lacks the stability it needs to stay firmly rooted is easily overtaken and destroyed. If you build a house on sand, how long will the house remain in place? How long will it be before it sinks, swallowed by the ground itself? The importance of a foundation is paramount for building a home that is not only successful, but also possesses longevity.

Our ancestors are our foundation. It is by their blood, sweat, tears, and sacrifices that you and I are able to stand where we are today. You see, they blazed the trail, fighting, cutting away the obstructions that block the road for each new generation that was (and is) birthed. The things they endured, the hardships they overcame, the challenges they faced as well as died for made it possible for us to continue to blaze that same trail. The trail I am referring to is the path of honoring your spirits and your family, and of doing what is right. It is also the path of wisdom, the path of work, and the path of forward movement. As the ancestors move forward, they do so with our help. You want to know how to serve the spirits? Begin with your ancestors.

Service to the Ancestors

Establishing a relationship with your ancestors is one of the most important things you could ever do. Knowing where you came from, the struggles of your people, and how they overcame carries with it the power to put the same principles to work in your own life, which, in turn, becomes a potent tool of strength within your work. It also opens the door to what will come. You see, you need to know where you came from to really know where you are going.

When I was a child, four years old to be exact, I was on a playground at one of the local parks. I was having a grand ole time going down the slide, climbing the little ladder to get back up to the top of it, and going down again. The feeling of being so high (in the mind of a four-year-old, twelve feet is like reaching the heavens) and sliding back down was out of this world! As I was sliding down, I began to hear something. It was music I had not heard before. I turned my head toward the direction of the music and saw a woman standing somewhat near the slide. She had a tambourine in her hand and it made the most amazing sounds! When I reached the bottom of the slide, I got up and made my way over to her. I couldn't stop staring as I was mesmerized by the sound and by the look she had on her face. It was as if I got lost in the beauty of what was happening.

She looked at me with eyes that were almost aflame and had a smile that felt like a grandmother's embrace. Then, she began to speak. She said to me that she was one of my people, an ancestor. She told me her name then went on to say that she was always with me and the power that was in my blood was the same power that was in hers. Now, in my opinion, a typical four-year-old would be utterly confused and possibly afraid of what was going on. I, on the other hand, was no typical four-year-old. I felt a strange comfort and security that I had never really felt before. She was my friend, after all.

She continued to speak to me and said that I needed to always remember to honor where I came from, to honor my blood, and that would lay the foundation of the trail I would blaze later on in my life. I didn't exactly know what all that meant, but I knew it was important. Then, my grandfather called my name. He was sitting on one of the wooden benches nearby, watching me play. I turned my head to acknowledge him and when I turned back to see her again, like a flash, she was gone. I told my grandfather about her and what she said. He then looked at me and told me that he knew who she was and that she was one of my protectors. He also said she came to me because I had a purpose and that our ancestors must always come first because they are our foundation.

It was at this point that I began to acknowledge, honor, and speak to my ancestors. In doing so I began to build an ancestral connection and a foundation that would become unshakable, not only in my work, but also in every aspect of my life. Now, how do we begin service to our ancestors? How do we begin to build that relationship and that foundation? Well, I'm going to tell you.

Our ancestors are very much like they were when they had bodies. They have opinions, feelings, and certainly hold wisdom and direction if we choose to receive it. The ancestors are great protectors of ours and, in my opinion, the greatest allies we can have. It should be no secret that the ancestors not only want to aid in our success, but also to help us weather life's storms. For this reason, there is a fundamental importance to their participation and direction in the things we do.

Now, I have seen and heard of all sorts of things regarding how you begin service to your ancestors. I have seen how complicated some folks make it and will tell you that it should not be that way, nor should it be contrived. The ancestors want a relationship with you—a relationship based on honor, love, and work. In this, as your heart grows toward them, so then does your sensitivity to them increase.

HONORING YOUR ANCESTORS

You begin very simply by inviting them into your home and your life, and asking for revelation. To start this work, you will want to have a few things:

- A space to do the work—it can be a tabletop or a shelf, wherever you prefer

- A white candle—a seven-day candle, one encased in glass that burns for seven continuous days, usually works well and helps to ease minds with regards to safety

- A glass of water

- Photographs of and personal items that belonged to your ancestors (if you don't have any, *name papers*—their names written down—will do fine)

- Some fresh fruit, for example, bananas, apples, grapes, or mangoes

- A plate on which to put the fruit

- A chair

The best time to begin this is right at dusk, when the transition of day to night is beginning and the door opens to more successful work.

Once you have made a space for them, begin by lighting the candle. A candle serves to light the way. It's kind of the same principle as the lighthouse that guides the ships toward the shore. The candle is also, in and of itself, an offering of elevation to your ancestors.

Once the candle is lit, present it to the four directions. Personally, I present it to the East, West, North, and South because that also symbolically represents the crossroads.

Why the crossroads? The crossroads is the meeting place of the physical and the spiritual. It is where both worlds come together and intersect, allowing both sides not only to meet, but also to commune with one another. The crossroads is one of the most powerful places in this world and, as such, should be honored and utilized by the spiritual person. When you think of the crossroads, you think of the potency of two places of power—the realm of the spirit and the realm of the physical that come together to commune. Here, in this communion, we see into the realm of the spirit and the realm of the spirit sees into the physical. To have this representation in the work with your ancestors will open it up even more because as we honor the power of the crossroads we honor the meeting place of the two worlds.

To present the candle to the four directions, the crossroads, you simply take the candle and hold it up in each direction. Begin in the East, then turn to the West, then to the North, and finally to the South. The sun rises in the East and represents newness, beginnings and the like. For that reason, we start in the East.

When you finish presenting to the four directions, put the candle down in the space you prepared for your ancestors.

Once the candle is placed on the space, go get the glass of water. Water is a conduit of the spirit, a means of travel, and a way of opening a door so the spirits can come through. We use water in this way when we are working with the spirits of our ancestors, not only to give them more access to come into our space, but also to serve as a key of sorts to the opening of the spiritual doors. When you have your glass of water, present it to the four directions as well, then place it in the space for your ancestors.

A very good friend of mine and fellow Conjure man, Candelo Kimbisa, talks about water and the ancestors. He and I were having a discussion about it and he said, "Always look for your ancestors in the water. The rain that falls now is the same rain that fell on our ancestors. It is a link to them and that link opens the door to their spirits. Whether it is by the river, in a rainstorm, or by the ocean, if you look for them, you will find them there." This is such a profound statement when you think about how the same water that touched your ancestors is now touching you. The fact that our bodies are comprised mostly of water and return to the earth when we leave them is something quite potent. The ancestors become part of that water again, you see.

The next thing you will want to do is to gather some personal things of your ancestors. Things like photographs, perhaps jewelry they wore, a piece of clothing that was theirs, or something that has a link to them. If you do not have photos and such, you can always use name papers. The important thing here is having something present that establishes a link to them. The link is part of what will facilitate communication, communion, and the opening of yourself to be able to receive the messages from the spirits themselves. Take the personal links of your ancestors and place them on the space, giving thanks to them by name as you set the items down.

The next thing is the food. The food is actually a very important part of this process. You see, even the dead have to eat. Food provides sustenance and energy for us to be able to do what we need to do. It is something that even the dead need as it gives them the energy to do work. They take the essence of the food, which has the ability to give energy, just as it does for the living. Aside from that, keep in mind that this process works very similarly to when your ancestors had bodies. Remember when folks would come over to your house or you would go to their house for a meal? The meal served as a tool that opened communication, establishing bonds and fostering relationships. For example, sitting around the dinner table, breaking bread with your relatives and talking about all sorts of things—you ate, drank, and experienced communion. Just because they no longer have bodies doesn't mean this aspect of service is any less important. The food also serves as nourishment—the living essence of the food nourishes and strengthens your ancestors to work for you as you simultaneously serve them.

So now, take the fruits you brought for them and put them on a plate. Lots of folks use white plates to symbolically represent an ancestral color. Personally, I do and I would suggest the same for you. You should also take a few pieces of the fruit and put them out by the front door as a means of welcoming your ancestors into your home. Consider it like giving them a gift before dinner or bringing a bottle of wine to the house. When that is done, take the plate of fruits and, yes again, present it to the four directions to give honor to the crossroads and also to send your work out to the four corners, both in the physical world and in the spirit. You will then put the plate down on the space and go grab the chair.

Everything should now be in place. When you get your chair, place it in front of the space and have a seat. This is when you will begin the process of calling out to your people, giving them thanks for who they are, for what they have done for you, and for the sacrifices they have made. These words are not just words, but also serve to open the door of your heart to those who came before you and to invite those hearing the call to make themselves known in a real way as an active part of your life.

The prayers to the ancestors do not have to be fancy. The prayers that come from your heart are the most potent. However, I will give an example of how I pray to my folks. It's something that holds the greatest importance for me because the ancestors are truly the foundation on which I stand. Here is an example:

I call out to you, ancestors, with words of thanksgiving, honor, and respect.

I thank you for everything you have done for me, for every sacrifice you have made, and for blazing the trail that I now stand on.

I honor you for who you are and for what you do.

Thank you for everything you have done for me and for everything you will do.

I ask that you come into this place, fill this place with your presence, and fill me with your wisdom and love.

Ancestors (you can call them by name here). I ask that you make me sensitive to your presence.

I ask that you reveal yourselves to me that I might know you, that I might know how you walked, that I might know the power of your work.

I ask you to open my ears to hear you, open my heart to know you, open my eyes to see you, open my hands to work with you, and open my feet to walk with you.

It is by your work and sacrifice that I am able to stand here now and I thank you for it! Thank you for all you have given me and for all you have done for me!

All I am and all I have come from you.

I give you honor, thanksgiving, and blessing!

You can continue to pray as long as you feel you should but don't half-ass the prayer. In other words, when you make your prayers, keep in mind that you are not just saying words, you are opening a door that brings on spiritual movement. If you just say something and there is nothing else involved other than uttering a word or two, do not expect good results. The more effort you give, the more revelation you receive. When you are finished with the prayers and thanksgiving to your ancestors, take a piece of fruit from the plate and eat with them. When you are eating, you should be listening. Listen for their voice, feel their presence, and be thankful. I get asked all the time how long the food should stay there. My answer is always the same—the food stays until they are done with it. Typically, their response is "how will I know?" My answer is "you will know."

There is something that happens with an offering when the spirits eat from it. The look and color change. It will look like the life that was in it is gone. For example, let's say that you give the ancestors some black coffee. You put it on their table, make your prayers, and begin talking to them. Then you tell them they have some coffee and to enjoy it. When you go back later, you may just discover that the black coffee you gave them looks different, almost a bit faded in color. You can absolutely tell that something got hold of it. It is at that point that the offering was accepted and they partook of what was given. They will let you know.

When they are finished with the food, do not throw it in the garbage, but take it outside to a nearby tree or bush and lay it there. The reason we do not throw it in the garbage is because we do not want to dishonor the offering given to them.

Now, this work is not a one-time deal. It is something that needs to be continued if it is to grow. Just like when you are exercising a muscle, the more you do it, the bigger it gets. This principle is the same for ancestor work. This work is not a once-a-year thing, contrary to some opinions. The more you work it, the more sensitive to them you become, the stronger you become, and the more you walk not only in your own wisdom, but also in the wisdom of those who came before you.

Feeding your ancestors needs to be a regular thing that you do with them. They should be fed at least once a week. Cook for them. Make a meal and eat with them. Do not put any salt in the food that you cook for them, because salt can send away the dead. Make things that they may have liked, if you know some of those foods. If you think this sounds like a lot of work, you would be correct. It *is* work. It is called spiritual *work* for a reason. It is not spiritual *easy*. The work that you continue to do with your ancestors works only to your own growth and benefit, so keep that in mind when you are doing these things.

You are the living temple of your ancestors. They reside in your blood. Whether you acknowledge it or not, you have a responsibility to honor that. The work of the ancestors is a life-long process that carries with it more blessings than you can imagine. It also carries with it a strength that is unmatched when it comes to your walk, your work, and your progression in this life. It is the power of the ancestors that enables us to stand in every single thing we do. It is the power of the ancestors that keeps us strong and able to withstand every storm of life that comes. When you have a strong relationship with your ancestors you become like a deep-rooted tree that could withstand the might of a hurricane, holding through whatever circumstances and conditions might try to uproot or destroy it.

Once you begin to establish a relationship with your ancestors, you will have access to wisdom and knowledge that you may not have known even existed. The ancestors can help you in every aspect of your life. Your spiritual work will increase and be more potent. Your physical life will improve. And when the storms of life come along, you will have an unshakable foundation that refuses to let you crumble. I cannot stress enough the importance of ancestral work and the foundational strength that you will receive from an active and thriving relationship with them.

In Conjure, this relationship is viewed as being of the utmost importance. One of the primary reasons for that is because you need to know where you came from in order to know where you are going. Why is that so? Well, when you know your ancestors, what they did, who they were, and how they lived, you get a road map of sorts that lends itself to your own progress and work that may need to be expanded upon.

Do you come from a family of healers? Do you come from a family of warriors? You see, these things are important because those gifts are in your blood. This is part of what I was referring to when I was talking about the wisdom of the ancestors in your life. Sometimes the lack of knowledge of those things can put those gifts into a stasis of sorts. Not all of the time, but you will be surprised at what you may have that you were not aware of.

The work of our ancestors should be evident in our work and what better way for that to happen than to go straight to them and gain that spiritual wisdom they possess? The ancestors can and do speak directly. You have a responsibility to be able to hear that voice and to answer that call. The trail they blazed for you is a part of your own spiritual walk and you must continue to walk and work. This is done by communion with your ancestors and receiving their wisdom. Remember, there is nothing you are going through or will go through that they haven't overcome in one way or another. So why wouldn't you want that wisdom in your arsenal? Not only does it make things more clear, but it also means that trying times have less probability of defeating you.

If you stand in the strength of your ancestors, you literally have an army at your side, and no matter what happens, you will never, ever have to go down the path of defeat. In one split second, the force of your ancestors can change a situation or circumstance and put right what is wrong. On the same note, your ancestors, who want you to move forward because you are their living representative, will give you the tools and assistance to take the good things of your life and work to make them better.

4

THE POWER OF THE ROOT

On a very warm summer's day, when I was a kid, I was outside in my backyard watching some work going on. There was a client of my grandfather's who came for some separation work. She was in a relationship that she no longer wanted but wouldn't actively leave. She had some fears about it and felt it would be better if her boyfriend took the initiative to separate from her. She was afraid that he might harm her, if she tried to leave him. She had brought with her a little of his hair, as well as a paper towel that held some of his semen. My grandfather took those personal items and made two small bags—one for the unwanted partner and one for her.

The bags were made by taking two small squares of cotton cloth and laying them both out on the table. A piece of the paper towel with the semen and the client's boyfriend's hair went on top of one of the squares of cloth, along with his full name written on a piece of paper and some Separation Powder (page 151).

The square intended for the client was very similar. It contained some of her hair, her full name on a piece of paper, and a few of her toenail clippings. When the items were placed on the squares, the corners of each cloth were gathered together and tied with some string. The string was wrapped around the corners of the cloth seven times, moving in the away direction.

Wrapping in an away direction means that you are wrapping so that the string moves away from you as it goes over the top of the bag as it is being closed up. You begin with the string underneath the bag. You then bring it to the top on the side closest to your body, and move it away from you over the top of the bag. Continue wrapping using this same motion until it has been wrapped the recommended number of times.

Once the wrapping was done, three knots were tied to close the cloths, creating a small bag. Wrapping in the away direction is to send work away from you, to repel something or somone. On a similar note, for work or jobs that are to draw something toward you (such as prosperity), you would wrap toward you. The number of times it was wrapped is the end or completion of a cycle, as is the number of knots that were tied.

As my grandfather was preparing the bags, he prayed over them. A candle was lit to illuminate the path and guide the work where it needed to go. When he finished making the bags, the client left the house. He kept the bags and continued to work.

We both walked outside, near the woods at the edge of the property. There was an area there where a lot of spiritual work is done. In this area grew a vine called kudzu. Kudzu grows insanely fast, sometimes almost a foot a day. You may have seen it for yourself in wooded areas that are overtaken with a viney-looking plant. We walked to a patch of kudzu and he began to make more prayers and declarations over the bags while I stood there with a lit candle in my hand.

The prayers and declarations were specific to the relationship of the client and her boyfriend. The separation of the two was coming, whether the boyfriend wanted it or not. When he finished the prayers and declarations, he took a bottle of whiskey and poured some on each of the bags. He then presented the bags, separately, to the four directions to send our work to the four corners of the earth. When he was finished, he poured a bit of the whiskey on two of the kudzu vines that were growing in separate directions. Once that was done, he tied one of the bags on the stem of one of the kudzu vines and the other on the stem of the vine growing in the opposite direction. After they were tied to their respective stems, he made more prayers and declarations to the spirits of the roots. Again, the declarations had everything to do with separation, leaving, growing apart, and the end of that relationship.

Once the prayers were complete, we walked away and left the work to continue on its own. The petitions had been made, the offerings given, the spirit of the roots had been asked to work, and the links belonging to the client and her boyfriend had been tied in such a way that separation would happen.

A week later, the client contacted my grandfather to tell him that the couple was arguing constantly, that her partner was calling her all sorts of bad names, and that he was treating her horribly. She was stressed and just wanted the whole thing to be over. My grandfather explained to her that this kind of work isn't pretty and that, due to its very nature, can produce heated and stressful circumstances. She understood and said she would continue to stand her ground, understanding that the work was progressing.

A month later, the client called my grandfather again, this time to tell him that the couple had split. Her partner had found someone else he wanted to be with and he was moving out. The client had experienced the end of a long and somewhat painful road, but it was done. For that, she was happy.

Work happens in various ways and she experienced what she needed, although not necessarily in the way she wanted. In this case, just as the two bags literally grew apart, so did the relationship and the man's desire to continue with it. The effect of the bags growing apart caused his change of mind and influenced him to end the relationship. The client's request was successful—and she also learned a lesson about being more discerning about who she became romantically involved with.

∞∞∞∞

One of the principles of Conjure and Hoodoo is that every plant and animal has a spirit. Each of these spirits has a predisposition toward some sort of work. The Bible, which absolutely does have a strong place in Conjure (a lot of us consider it an old spell book, actually), says in Genesis 1:29, "And God said, Behold, I have given you every herb bearing seed, which is upon the face of all the earth, and every tree, in the which is the fruit of a tree yielding seed; to you it shall be for meat."

The word *meat* as used here here has multiple meanings. One of them, of course, is to eat or consume. This act alone creates sustenance and enables us to continue to function, to work. Another meaning of the word is that it is fuel. This fuel has been associated with fire, as in kindling as such, but also carries with it connotations of work or using the fire for work.

Depending on the specific plant, whether root, flower, or leaf, botanicals have many different and individual uses. However, each of them will fuel something. Some plants bring healing, while others bring death. The variations are many and there are countless ways that plants might be worked with. The truth in this becomes apparent when we examine roots and the powers they possess. Like every other living being, each root has its own personality. Some run hot, while others are more subtle and soothing. When you are going to work with them you need to understand their personality, their spirit.

For example, cinnamon has some kick to it. The spirit of cinnamon is strong and hot. Taste it and you will know exactly what I mean. When you use cinnamon in work, you are adding heat and potency to whatever you are doing. Cinnamon's spiciness has a heat that can burn away superficial foolishness, remove some blockages, draw money, and let inner passions rise. This is why cinnamon is so beneficial in works of love, lust, luck, money, and in some cases heated domination. Heated domination would be a more assertive and aggressive type of domination work. But cinnamon also has a subtle sweetness to its aroma that evokes passion and creates a *drawing* effect, especially in the areas of relationships and money. When I talk about drawing, I am referring to attracting something. Just as a magnet draws or pulls things to it, the same is true when it comes to drawing works.

A relationship with the roots is something that you must have if you are going to be, or call yourself, a worker. A good part of our work and its power comes from that relationship and the connection we have with the spirit of the root, much like the relationship we have with our ancestors and other spirits.

This confuses some folks because they don't comprehend the concept that somebody can have a relationship with a bay leaf. It's important that you look at it from the perspective of having a working relationship with another spirit because that's exactly what it is. The spirits of the roots are no different from any other spirit and this work must be held in such a way that it becomes the catalyst that produces the results.

There are so many things that can be done with the roots that it would make your head spin if it weren't glued on. The power of the roots can bring love, harness control, draw money and luck, as well as destroy, curse, and close down every opportunity you thought you had. When you think of how many things can happen with the roots, it's something that is not only awe inspiring, but also can inspire fear.

∞∞∞

Did you know that I can take a few things, such as rue, hyssop, and agrimony, and use them to remove any and all things that have blocked you, shut down your crossroads, and tainted your spirit?

A CLEANSING BATH FOR CLEARING AWAY BLOCKS

With these three roots, a bath and dressing of the head will suck the bad luck and negativity from your life. Just as the yoke is taken from the ox, so is the yoke that weighs you down destroyed and the heaviness lifted. *NOTE: If you have herbal allergies it would not be wise to take a bath with the roots.*

Ingredients:

- 1 white candle, plus one more for the bath
- A glass of water
- A plate
- 1 handful of hyssop (*Hyssopus officinalis*)
- 1 handful of rue (*Ruta graveolens*)
- 1 handful of agrimony (*Agrimonia eupatoria*)
- Cigar or cigarette for smoke
- Rum or whiskey
- A medium-size pot

- Enough water to fill the pot

- A few dabs of Florida Water

- Warm water for the bath

- A white cloth or bandana for your head

- White or light-colored clothing to wear to bed

First, get a candle and a glass of water.

Then, take those roots and set them on a plate.

Light the candle and present it with the roots (hyssop, rue, and agrimony) to the four directions to send out your work to the four corners of the world.

Once that's done, you're going to begin to pray over them. One of my favorite prayers for this kind of work is Psalm 91:

91 He that dwelleth in the secret place of the most High shall abide under the shadow of the Almighty.

2 I will say of the Lord, He is my refuge and my fortress: my God; in him will I trust.

3 Surely he shall deliver thee from the snare of the fowler, and from the noisome pestilence.

4 He shall cover thee with his feathers, and under his wings shalt thou trust: his truth shall be thy shield and buckler.

5 Thou shalt not be afraid for the terror by night; nor for the arrow that flieth by day;

6 Nor for the pestilence that walketh in darkness; nor for the destruction that wasteth at noonday.

7 A THOUSAND SHALL FALL AT THY SIDE, AND TEN THOUSAND AT THY RIGHT HAND; BUT IT SHALL NOT COME NIGH THEE.

8 ONLY WITH THINE EYES SHALT THOU BEHOLD AND SEE THE REWARD OF THE WICKED.

9 BECAUSE THOU HAST MADE THE LORD, WHICH IS MY REFUGE, EVEN THE MOST HIGH, THY HABITATION;

10 THERE SHALL NO EVIL BEFALL THEE, NEITHER SHALL ANY PLAGUE COME NIGH THY DWELLING.

11 FOR HE SHALL GIVE HIS ANGELS CHARGE OVER THEE, TO KEEP THEE IN ALL THY WAYS.

12 THEY SHALL BEAR THEE UP IN THEIR HANDS, LEST THOU DASH THY FOOT AGAINST A STONE.

13 THOU SHALT TREAD UPON THE LION AND ADDER: THE YOUNG LION AND THE DRAGON SHALT THOU TRAMPLE UNDER FEET.

14 BECAUSE HE HATH SET HIS LOVE UPON ME, THERE-FORE WILL I DELIVER HIM: I WILL SET HIM ON HIGH, BECAUSE HE HATH KNOWN MY NAME.

15 HE SHALL CALL UPON ME, AND I WILL ANSWER HIM: I WILL BE WITH HIM IN TROUBLE; I WILL DELIVER HIM, AND HONOUR HIM.

16 WITH LONG LIFE WILL I SATISFY HIM, AND SHEW HIM MY SALVATION.

The second Psalm to pray is Psalm 51. Now, this is a Psalm of repentance, so why are we doing this? The reason is, there are always things we have done in our lives that render negative buildup or are counterproductive to our moving forward, receiving blessings, and prospering in the everyday aspects of our lives. The work of this Psalm brings cleansing and renewal. For that reason, it is important. Now, pray over the roots with Psalm 51:

51 HAVE MERCY UPON ME, O GOD, ACCORDING TO THY LOV-INGKINDNESS: ACCORDING UNTO THE MULTITUDE OF THY TENDER MERCIES BLOT OUT MY TRANSGRESSIONS.

2 WASH ME THROUGHLY FROM MINE INIQUITY, AND CLEANSE ME FROM MY SIN.

3 FOR I ACKNOWLEDGE MY TRANSGRESSIONS: AND MY SIN IS EVER BEFORE ME.

4 AGAINST THEE, THEE ONLY, HAVE I SINNED, AND DONE THIS EVIL IN THY SIGHT: THAT THOU MIGHTEST BE JUSTIFIED WHEN THOU SPEAKEST, AND BE CLEAR WHEN THOU JUDGEST.

5 BEHOLD, I WAS SHAPEN IN INIQUITY; AND IN SIN DID MY MOTHER CONCEIVE ME.

6 BEHOLD, THOU DESIREST TRUTH IN THE INWARD PARTS: AND IN THE HIDDEN PART THOU SHALT MAKE ME TO KNOW WISDOM.

7 PURGE ME WITH HYSSOP, AND I SHALL BE CLEAN: WASH ME, AND I SHALL BE WHITER THAN SNOW.

8 MAKE ME TO HEAR JOY AND GLADNESS; THAT THE BONES WHICH THOU HAST BROKEN MAY REJOICE.

9 HIDE THY FACE FROM MY SINS, AND BLOT OUT ALL MINE INIQUITIES.

10 CREATE IN ME A CLEAN HEART, O GOD; AND RENEW A RIGHT SPIRIT WITHIN ME.

11 CAST ME NOT AWAY FROM THY PRESENCE; AND TAKE NOT THY HOLY SPIRIT FROM ME.

12 RESTORE UNTO ME THE JOY OF THY SALVATION; AND UPHOLD ME WITH THY FREE SPIRIT.

13 THEN WILL I TEACH TRANSGRESSORS THY WAYS; AND SINNERS SHALL BE CONVERTED UNTO THEE.

14 DELIVER ME FROM BLOODGUILTINESS, O GOD, THOU GOD OF MY SALVATION: AND MY TONGUE SHALL SING ALOUD OF THY RIGHTEOUSNESS.

15 O LORD, OPEN THOU MY LIPS; AND MY MOUTH SHALL SHEW FORTH THY PRAISE.

16 FOR THOU DESIREST NOT SACRIFICE; ELSE WOULD I GIVE IT: THOU DELIGHTEST NOT IN BURNT OFFERING.

17 THE SACRIFICES OF GOD ARE A BROKEN SPIRIT: A BROKEN AND A CONTRITE HEART, O GOD, THOU WILT NOT DESPISE.

18 DO GOOD IN THY GOOD PLEASURE UNTO ZION: BUILD THOU THE WALLS OF JERUSALEM.

19 THEN SHALT THOU BE PLEASED WITH THE SACRIFICES OF RIGHTEOUSNESS, WITH BURNT OFFERING AND WHOLE BURNT OFFERING: THEN SHALL THEY OFFER BULLOCKS UPON THINE ALTAR.

When you are making these prayers, you need to apply them to yourself. You are asking the roots to do the work to cleanse you, to renew you, and to empower you. Don't get caught up in simply reading the words, but feel them, feel the power, understand the work that is about to go down. Continue with prayers of thanksgiving for the work that is happening, for the roots that will labor to make the spiritual change that will reflect into the physical world, for the magical transformation that's going to leave you full of power, clean, and vibrating with the potency of the spirit!

Once the prayers are made, give the roots some smoke and some rum or whiskey. To offer smoke, first, light a cigar or cigarette (the cigar is especially good for this). Next, put the lit end in your mouth and blow through the cigar onto the roots. The offerings given are a token of payment for the roots to aid in the work, so they are important.

Next you are going to get the pot and put some water in it. Put it on the stove and turn on the heat.

As the water is heating up, put a few dabs of Florida Water in it. Florida Water is a cologne that has been around since the 1800s that has become a staple in a worker's arsenal. It is very, very good for spiritual cleansing and removing the muck that holds you back and creates blockages. It can also be used as an ancestral offering when you light it on fire.

During this process, you want to continue making declarations of your cleansing and your renewal. "I will be cleansed and nothing will block me." "My spirit is renewed and my roads are open." Declarations such as these will do you and the work good.

When the water heats up, put a handful of each of the roots in the pot and let it boil a few minutes. After it's been boiling about five minutes, turn off the stove.

Go and get the second white candle and put it in the bathroom by the tub.

Draw a bath and make sure the water is very warm.

Scoop out about three-quarters of the roots that are in the pot and put them back on the plate. Take them into the bathroom and set them near the candle.

Take the pot to the bathroom, pour it in the tub, and stir it up. Once you've done that, you can get in the tub.

When you are in the tub you're going to begin to wash yourself, from the head downward—only in a downward motion.

While you're washing, you will continue to make those prayers and petitions for your cleansing, your renewal, and your restoration. You need to be in the tub for about ten to fifteen minutes, washing downward and making those declarations.

Once you have finished washing yourself, go ahead and let the water out of the tub. Now, there are folks who say you can towel dry and folks who say you need to drip-dry. I come from the school of drip-drying because you want those roots to soak into your skin. You don't want to wipe it off. After you've drip-dried for a few minutes you can certainly take a towel and dab yourself in wet areas.

When you're done with that, take the roots that are on the plate and put them on your head. Once they are there, take a white cloth (a white bandana works great) and wrap and tie it around your head so the roots stay there.

Next put on some white or light-colored clothing and sleep with the covering on your head. The next morning you can shower and wash your hair.

This needs to be done for three days in a row. You cannot break the chain of the work. If you skip a day, you have to start over again. Conjure works in cycles, so you have to do all of it if you want to work it right.

After you have finished the third day, watch and see how you feel and you will know exactly how potent the roots are.

ooooo

One of the reasons for the potency we have in Conjure is because of this working relationship. I speak to the roots just as I do with my other spirits. I also honor them in the same way. As you are working with the knowledge that you need to build a relationship with the spirit of the roots, there is power there that comes. The relationship is the foundation and the power is built from that. Power that not only will change your work and make it more potent, but also change the way you see the roots and even your own life.

The way I was taught to establish relationship with the roots is the same way I was taught to establish relationship with my ancestors. You take the roots and make prayers to them, you give thanks to them, elevating them with words of edification and strength. You give them offerings such as smoke, rum or whiskey, water, light, even coins. You have songs to sing for them. As you continue to do these things with them, they respond back to you and are more ready and willing to execute the work that will follow. Remember, it's always easier to ask a friend for help than a stranger.

Begin by simply talking to the roots. What roots? Well, everyone has roots and herbs around their house. Look in your kitchen cabinet; I bet you'll find some there. Pick three of them. Feel them and touch them, ask them to reveal their spirits to you, and see what happens. Don't come to me and tell me that you did it once and nothing happened. It is a door you will have to knock on more than once for it to begin to work. Persistence, dedication, and faith are all a part of this work and if you have none of those things then it's not going to serve you.

After a bit, you will see that door begin to open and when it does, a whole new world will reveal itself to you. A world that shows you primal power and holds within it keys to working magic in a way you may not have been aware of. The power of the root is always there, but most of the time, we are the problem when it comes to being able to recognize and feel it. The more you knock at the door the more likely it is the door will open and the primal power of the root will become something that you can work with and for. The roots hold within themselves the power of the earth, the power of the heavens, and the power of the elements. Their very nature is both creative and destructive because you have to have both for balance.

5

THE POWER OF THE DIRT

Conjure is a tradition with tremendous power that comes from the earth itself. The earth is literally alive and holds within it spirits, secrets, and magical potency that has always been quite formidable. When you think about it, the power held within the earth is something that has been used for millennia. The dirt of the earth houses the bodies of our ancestors. The dirt of the earth creates life as things are planted and new growth forms. Things are built on the dirt of the earth, which becomes a foundation that houses the spirit of place and establishes a tangible structure for ceremony. The spirit of the earth itself not only absorbs power, but also gives it in return. As the cycle of life is birth, life, death, and life again, so it is that the power of the earth both absorbs and emanates spiritual potency.

I was speaking with my good friend, fellow Conjure worker and author Starr Casas. We were discussing the power of the root and the power of the earth. As she and I were talking, she had what we call an utterance of the spirit. An utterance of the spirit is divine knowledge that is spoken to create revelation. She said, "Most folks don't understand that the power of the root and dirt comes from the ancestors buried deep within the land. The power of their blood and bones mingles with the earth and draws forth the power of the roots that grow there. As the root lived, so shall it die and live again."

This comment just about made me fall out of my chair when I heard it. The ring of truth to it was absolute and the power that sat with those words was something that only the spirit could reveal. The power of the ancestors feeds the earth as they (and we) return to it. The connection of the spirit to the earth is something that shows the working relationship we have with both. You need not only to have success, but also to work in such a way that you are effective in every facet of your life. The connection is there; you just have to open your mind to it. As the ancestors feed the dirt, we use the dirt in our work.

Dirts vary in what and how they are used. The individual spirit of place in each established area is what you want to look at. What is built on that particular piece of land? How is the place used? What goes on there? The absorbing side of the earth will take those spirits, those essences into itself and guess what? You will have a concentrated power that is latent in those dirts.

A MOJO HAND FOR MONEY AND PROSPERITY

Let's take prosperity work for example.

Ingredients:

- 2 pinches of thyme (*Thymus vulgaris*)—used in prosperity work to bring money to you

- 1 pinch of cinnamon (*Cinnamomum spp*)—used to heat up work and has potency when it comes to raising passions and drawing money

- A magnet—used to draw money in our direction

- 1 orange peel (*Citrus reticulata*)—used for prosperity work and for opening up doors of financial gain

- 1 High John the Conqueror root (*Convolvulus jalapa*)—used for its power to bust through obstacles and remove blockages

- 3 black-eyed peas—used in works of prosperity and financial stability (three to complete a cycle and to honor the Holy Trinity)

- 1 dollar bill or similar paper money from other currencies—used as the focus of what you are going to draw to you

- A plate

- A candle

- A glass of water

- Rum or whiskey

- A cigar for smoke

- A piece of green or gold flannel or cotton cloth, approximately 4–6 inches in size

- 18" of cotton string—used to tie the hand together—do *not* cut the string with scissors or a blade, as it can sever the work; use a candle flame to burn the string and split it from the roll

- A trowel

- A few coins

- A few drops of rum or whiskey

- A few drops of an oil (Allspice Oil works well for prosperity and money drawing)

Allspice Oil

- About ½ a Mason jar of allspice (*Pimenta dioica*)
- About ½ a Mason jar of olive oil

Allspice Oil Instructions

Take equal parts of the allspice and olive oil and put them in a Mason jar. I like to use Mason jars because they have a strong seal on them.

Next, warm the oil. A good way to do this is to put some water in a slow cooker and turn it on low, then put the filled jar inside and let it simmer for a couple of days.

When it's done, take the jar out and store it in a dark place. Give the olive oil about a month to meld with the allspice.

MOJO HAND INSTRUCTIONS

Take the roots and put them on a plate together.

Light the candle to illuminate the path of the work.

Set the glass of water down on the work space.

Take a cigar and some rum or whiskey and give the roots some smoke and liquor. You can use other liquors if you like. I use rum or whiskey because that is how I was raised and I have always gotten the best response to the work from those offerings.

Now take the plate of roots and ingredients and present it to the four directions. Once that is done, begin to make your prayers and declarations over the roots. A great prayer to use comes from Deuteronomy 28:1–13:

28 And it shall come to pass, if thou shalt hearken diligently unto the voice of the Lord thy God, to observe and to do all his commandments which I command thee this day, that the Lord thy God will set thee on high above all nations of the earth:

2 And all these blessings shall come on thee, and overtake thee, if thou shalt hearken unto the voice of the Lord thy God.

3 Blessed shalt thou be in the city, and blessed shalt thou be in the field.

4 Blessed shall be the fruit of thy body, and the fruit of thy ground, and the fruit of thy cattle, the increase of thy kine, and the flocks of thy sheep.

5 Blessed shall be thy basket and thy store.

6 Blessed shalt thou be when thou comest in, and blessed shalt thou be when thou goest out.

7 The Lord shall cause thine enemies that rise up against thee to be smitten before thy face: they shall come out against thee one way, and flee before thee seven ways.

8 The Lord shall command the blessing upon thee in thy storehouses, and in all that thou settest thine hand unto; and he shall bless thee in the land which the Lord thy God giveth thee.

9 The Lord shall establish thee an holy people unto himself, as he hath sworn unto thee, if thou shalt keep the commandments of the Lord thy God, and walk in his ways.

10 AND ALL PEOPLE OF THE EARTH SHALL SEE THAT
THOU ART CALLED BY THE NAME OF THE LORD; AND
THEY SHALL BE AFRAID OF THEE.

11 AND THE LORD SHALL MAKE THEE PLENTEOUS IN
GOODS, IN THE FRUIT OF THY BODY, AND IN THE FRUIT OF
THY CATTLE, AND IN THE FRUIT OF THY GROUND, IN THE
LAND WHICH THE LORD SWARE UNTO THY FATHERS TO
GIVE THEE.

12 THE LORD SHALL OPEN UNTO THEE HIS GOOD TREA-
SURE, THE HEAVEN TO GIVE THE RAIN UNTO THY LAND
IN HIS SEASON, AND TO BLESS ALL THE WORK OF THINE
HAND: AND THOU SHALT LEND UNTO MANY NATIONS, AND
THOU SHALT NOT BORROW.

13 AND THE LORD SHALL MAKE THEE THE HEAD, AND
NOT THE TAIL; AND THOU SHALT BE ABOVE ONLY, AND
THOU SHALT NOT BE BENEATH; IF THAT THOU HEARKEN
UNTO THE COMMANDMENTS OF THE LORD THY GOD,
WHICH I COMMAND THEE THIS DAY, TO OBSERVE AND TO
DO THEM:

This is a powerful prayer/declaration when doing prosperity or money-drawing work. It is important to make sure that
you apply the prayer to yourself and to your work. You can and
should also make declarations of your own. Declarations of your
own would include prayers, statements of direction for the job
to be done, as well as utterances of edification and clarity to the
roots and the ancestors. Never forget that the ancestors are
the foundation for all that we do. For example:

I COME TO THE SPIRITS OF THE ROOTS, STANDING ON THE
FOUNDATION OF MY ANCESTORS. I GIVE THANKS FOR ALL
THAT YOU HAVE DONE FOR ME AND FOR ALL THAT YOU

ARE GOING TO DO. I ASK THAT THE SPIRITS OF THE ROOTS
RISE UP AND DO THIS JOB FOR ME. I ASK THAT THIS WORK
OF PROSPERITY BE ONE THAT DRAWS MONEY, BLESSINGS,
AND OPPORTUNITY MY WAY. ANCESTORS, PLEASE GIVE
ME THE STRENGTH TO PRAY THIS WORK INTO POWER, TO
STAND IN ALL THINGS AND OVERCOME IN EVERY WAY. FOR
THAT, I HONOR YOU AND GIVE YOU ALL THANKS. SPIRITS OF
THE ROOTS, COME TOGETHER TO EMPOWER THIS HAND
SO THAT MONEY AND PROSPERITY ARE DRAWN TO ME.
EMPOWER THIS HAND SO THAT MONEY AND PROSPERITY
FOLLOW ME IN ALL THAT I DO AND IN EVERY PLACE THAT
I GO. I GIVE YOU THANKS FOR THE JOB YOU ARE ABOUT TO
DO AND I HONOR YOU IN ALL THINGS. AMEN.

What's important here is that you are making the petitions
to the roots for the work.

After your prayers and petitions have been made, take a good-
size pinch of each of the roots and place it in the center of the
piece of cloth. While doing this, speak to each of the ingredients individually. For example, "Cinnamon, be a fire in this work
to bring prosperity to me." "Thyme, draw money in my direction
and let my hands be blessed to receive it." Speaking to the roots
and assigning them their jobs is important in both the working
relationship of the root in Conjure and in providing a focus for
what you need to have done.

Once this has been accomplished, take the piece of cloth with
all the ingredients on it and gather the corners of it together.
When the corners have been gathered together it will resemble
a little bag.

When your string is ready and you have the corners gathered,
begin to wrap it, right above the top of the ingredients so the
bag is tight and everything is close together. You want to wrap

it toward you seven times to draw prosperity to you, continuing to make those prayers and declarations of prosperity and money coming your way. Once you have finished wrapping the bag, you are going to tie three knots in the string. Make sure they are good and tight so nothing falls out or gets loose.

Now that this part is finished, it's time to take a trip to the bank. Why the bank? The bank is a place where the focus is on money. The spirit of that place is one of money changing hands and, if you think about it, it is a magnet that draws money to it. Once you get there, you may have to be a little bit of a ninja (inconspicuous) because most folks probably won't understand what you are about to do. Find a place at the bank where you can dig a little hole. Usually, somewhere on the property of the bank there is some sort of grass, dirt, and the like, where the hole can be opened up. Dig the hole and place some coins in it as an offering to pay for the work that this dirt is about to help you with.

When you drop the coins in the hole, put the bag on top of them and cover it up. The bag should now be buried. Then, make more prayers and declarations there and when you're finished you can leave. The bag is now in the proverbial oven, cooking and soaking up some of those good money juices.

Once it has been buried for three days, you can go and dig it up. The importance of keeping it buried for that time is to allow it to absorb some of the place's essence. Being buried in the earth of a money-drawing place gives it power to help it do the job it was made to do. As the power of the dirt holds essences of money and drawing of the same, so then does the mojo hand that is buried there absorb those potencies. See, this is why folks will hear me say (and have time and time again), throwing roots in a bag a mojo hand does not make. This is work and if you want it to work then you have to work for it. It's quite simple.

After it has been dug up you can dress it with a few drops of rum or whiskey and Allspice Oil (page 50).

Now, you have a hot working mojo hand that is ready to draw some money and prosperity your way. Carry it on your person and let the magnetic pull start pulling! Trust and believe you will be surprised at how well the hand works.

ooooo

So then, understanding that dirts hold power as well as spirit and they are used in Conjure to do work just as the roots are, you can see that there is potency in the earth. Different sorts of places hold different and distinctive powers and potencies. Here is a list of a few dirts you may find helpful:

- Banks—money drawing, prosperity, transactions that involve finance
- Casinos—luck, but may also be used in work to bring out or encourage someone's addiction
- Courthouse—justice work and influence in matters of criminal and civil litigation
- Post Office—communication work
- Hospital—healing work
- College—work to bring opportunity and understanding
- River—drawing, removing, and sending away work
- Ocean—creation, cleansing, and fertility work; sand is the dirt of the ocean; even though it is not technically dirt, the essense of the ocean is there
- Graveyard—works with the dead, both positive and negative, revenge, protection, healing, and works of spirit sensitivity (work that is done to make one more sensitive to the spirit); this complex power differs between grave-yards and within the graveyards themselves

These are but a few examples. It's crucial to understand the various spirits of place. Dirts may also be added to mojo hands, powders, oils, and other workings to strengthen and enhance their power. To understand the spirit of a place is to understand the spirit of the dirt itself.

The power of the earth possesses many different aspects. When you begin to understand these aspects, you begin to build an even more powerful repertoire, which holds within it a key to effective Conjure work. When the arsenal has a lot of ammunition, there's no need to worry about running out of bullets. Remember, though, that we came from the dust of the earth and to it we are going to return. Well, our bodies will, anyway. A Conjure worker always has his or her hands in the dirt in one way or another. Building a relationship with the spirits of the dirts will open you up to becoming a well-rounded worker who is focused on the Conjure life and, with it, the work of the ancestors that came before you and the continuation of that work after you. In other words, the more you work, the more you have relationships with your ancestors and understand the spirit of the roots, the more balanced you will be in this work and in its amazing benefits.

That being said, there are times in our lives when we all need some sort of healing. I am going to give you a simple work for healing. This work can be done for yourself, a loved one, or someone else who has a need.

A SIMPLE WORK FOR HEALING

Ingredients:

- A few coins for when you gather the dirts

- 1 candle for lighting the path, plus 7 white candles—1 for each day of the work
- A glass of water
- A plate
- 2 pinches of dirt from a hospital
- 2 pinches of dirt from a river or ocean (sand)
- 1 pinch of hyssop
- 1 pinch Life Everlasting (*Helichrysum stoechas*)
- 1 pinch Master of the Woods (*Asperula odorata*)
- An angelica root (*Angelica archangelica*)
- 1 pinch of calendula (*Calendula officinalis*)
- A cigar for smoke
- Rum or whiskey
- A new pin or needle that has never been used
- About a tablespoon of olive oil
- A bowl (medium to large size)
- A photo of the person that needs healing

Remember, when you are collecting your dirts, that you need to pay for them, so leave some coins at the locations where you obtain them. Once you have your dirts and the other roots, you are going to bring them back to the space where you are going to do the work.

As with everything, you are going to light a candle and get a glass of water to begin.

Once you have done this, go ahead and put the dirts and roots on a plate.

Make your offerings of smoke and rum or whiskey, present everything to the four directions, and begin to make your prayers over the roots.

While you are making your prayers and petitions, make sure to call the person who needs healing by name in those utterances. In other words, name the individual in your prayers. While you are making your prayers and petitions, be specific as to the individual it is for. I like to recite Psalm 107:10–22 for healing:

10 SUCH AS SIT IN DARKNESS AND IN THE SHADOW OF DEATH, BEING BOUND IN AFFLICTION AND IRON;

11 BECAUSE THEY REBELLED AGAINST THE WORDS OF GOD, AND CONTEMNED THE COUNSEL OF THE MOST HIGH:

12 THEREFORE HE BROUGHT DOWN THEIR HEART WITH LABOUR; THEY FELL DOWN, AND THERE WAS NONE TO HELP.

13 THEN THEY CRIED UNTO THE LORD IN THEIR TROUBLE, AND HE SAVED THEM OUT OF THEIR DISTRESSES.

14 HE BROUGHT THEM OUT OF DARKNESS AND THE SHADOW OF DEATH, AND BRAKE THEIR BANDS IN SUNDER.

15 OH THAT MEN WOULD PRAISE THE LORD FOR HIS GOODNESS, AND FOR HIS WONDERFUL WORKS TO THE CHILDREN OF MEN!

16 FOR HE HATH BROKEN THE GATES OF BRASS, AND CUT THE BARS OF IRON IN SUNDER.

17 FOOLS BECAUSE OF THEIR TRANSGRESSION, AND BECAUSE OF THEIR INIQUITIES, ARE AFFLICTED.

18 THEIR SOUL ABHORRETH ALL MANNER OF MEAT; AND THEY DRAW NEAR UNTO THE GATES OF DEATH.

19 Then they cry unto the Lord in their trouble, and he saveth them out of their distresses.

20 He sent his word, and healed them, and delivered them from their destructions.

21 Oh that men would praise the Lord for his goodness, and for his wonderful works to the children of men!

22 And let them sacrifice the sacrifices of thanksgiving, and declare his works with rejoicing.

Repeat this Psalm three times. It is a great prayer and declaration to make for healing.

Make your prayers, petitions, and offerings, then take the needle or pin and carve the individual's name into one candle, making declarations of healing on their behalf as you are doing it. You can also use a nail if needed for this. This is also a good time to be asking your ancestors for aid and wisdom in your work. Remember, do *not* use a knife to carve into the candle so it doesn't cut away or sever the work.

After the name has been carved, rub a bit of olive oil on the candle, including the carved name. Olive oil is beneficial for peace and stability and will also serve as a fuel to make that candle burn hotter. Healing should be soothing, yes, but it should also be hot work to burn away the affliction.

Now, you are going to bring together all of the roots and dirts and put them in the bowl. Mix them up with your hand, making declarations of healing power and the freeing of the bonds of affliction for the individual.

Take the photograph of the person who needs healing and add it to the mix. It doesn't need to be at the very bottom of the bowl, but should be surrounded by the healing mix on all sides.

When this has been accomplished, take the carved candle and place it atop the photo in the bowl. Just as you would put a stake in the ground, you will plant the candle in the bowl.

Once the candle is set, you can go ahead and light it. Continue to make your prayers and petitions over the work that you are doing, uttering declarations of healing and the release of whatever the condition is. The work can be placed at your ancestor altar for additional aid in getting the healing done.

Repeat this work for a minimum of seven days (a completion of a cycle, in this case, healing), which is why it requires seven candles. Each day, carve, oil, set, and light a new candle and continue to make those declarations, prayers, and petitions over that work so the healing can flow to the person in need.

This is another example of how to use the power of the dirt to work spiritual and physical change in someone's life. Conjure is all about the magical potency of the dirt, especially when it comes to getting the job done and done well.

6

BALANCE IN WORKING CONJURE

Some magical practitioners frequently herald the principle that any and all work should be positive or "do no harm."

We hear the terms *black magic* and *white magic* thrown around as if to define the work by a color or by that which is generally accepted as being good or evil, positive or negative. The terms *good* and *evil* are relative. What one culture considers to be morally acceptable or good may not be considered the same in another culture.

I came upon the teaching that magic and spiritual work are one constant that cannot be accurately described as any color or intent but rather as a force that creates change. The important thing to note about the use of Conjure as a magical practice is that balance is the primary key—not perceived good or evil.

For example, you are in your house, asleep. Then, all of a sudden, you hear the sound of glass breaking from one of the windows in another room. Your family is there, awakened by the sound of an intruder entering your home. The only thing that runs through your mind is, "What are they going to do to me and my family?" Do you go out and greet the intruder with a blessing? Do you walk up to them and say, "Everything I have is yours, if you like?" How would that be welcomed, I wonder. Maybe, if you are lucky, the intruder would take only some of your belongings and not harm you or your family. This, of course, would be the best possible case. I submit that most anyone would do what is necessary to defend themselves and their family until the threat is neutralized. In this scenario, an offense is committed against you by the intruder breaking into your home. It is returned with an offense to stop further acts against you and to make damn sure the threat ceases to exist. Trust and believe that if I were the one involved, they might get in, but they won't get out.

The same basic principle is applied to magic and spiritual work. When offenses are worked against you, they should be returned. Otherwise, balance is not maintained and you end up becoming the victim of any and every work that may be done against you. In Conjure, we learn how to bless, heal, trick, curse, and eliminate. The basic understanding of these works is that they are all necessary, because they balance one another out when used with justice, wisdom, and responsibility as the deciding factors as to what is or is not to be done.

This principle can be found in the very roots we work with. Take the rose, for example. Its petals are an amazing attractant and are quite often used in love work. The spirit of the petals has a way of opening the eyes of the individual using them so that they may see themselves as the beauty they are. The petals also draw those who are looking for love to the person for whom the work is done. The petals can be used in hands, candle work, as well as baths.

On the other side of the coin, however, the rose also has thorns. Now, how could something so beautiful and full of love also have something that can pierce and hurt? This is the balance of the root. The thorns are used to take love away, to pierce and puncture a love, and to create discord. Some will say that the thorns are used to protect the love the petals have drawn. That is one theory, but the piercing side of the thorns has a spirit that is not exactly there to protect. The spirit of the thorns is used to tear away. These acts are for break-up work, particularly the breakup of a relationship. We have all heard the phrase "love hurts" a time or two, I would imagine. The thorns are the hurting side of love because that is their spirit.

So, when we talk about working in balance, it is a matter of seeing both sides of the coin. Sometimes the path that is not so heavily traveled is the one that is needed because, even in the midst of what could be construed as cursing, destruction, trick laying, or hexing, a creation is born to bring about restoration. Whether it is the creation of a new starting point, the protection of yourself or loved ones, the tearing down of an individual so they can rebuild themselves, or the removal of something entirely out of your life so you can see the road more clearly, these principles stand to do what is necessary to keep or restore the balance.

Just as nature possesses the power to both create and destroy, so does the work that we do. Now, am I saying that you just need to go around laying tricks, dropping powders, and working curses? Absolutely not. What I am saying is that every work, whether positive or negative, must be *balanced*. In order to have that balance, you have to know how to work with both hands.

The way I was raised, it is the responsibility of the worker to be able to see the balance in things, to have a relationship with their spirits that brings wisdom to the Conjure man or Conjure woman, and to do the work that is necessary to create the change that is called for at the time.

How do we see the balance of things, so we know how to do the work? When workers are born, there is an innate gift, a sensitivity to things that opens the door to be able to see the bigger picture. This gift is cultivated by relationship with your ancestors and your spirits, and the service given to them. As the crossroads brings together the spiritual and the physical, so does the gift of the worker open the ability to see, to prescribe and to perform work that opens the path of the bigger picture so that the goal is met. The workers who have strong relationships with their spirits are the workers who can walk the path of the crossroads to make the change that is balanced with work that is effective, potent, and overcomes adversities.

I had a client once who came to me seeking revenge work against her ex-lover. She told me all sorts of things about how he was so horrible to her. She told me that he didn't pay attention to her, that he always put his friends and his work before her, and that he ended the relationship because he did not feel like they were moving forward as a couple and that he wanted to focus on himself for a while. She also described him as controlling because he never let her do what she wanted to do. She was very adamant that she had been done wrong in their relationship and wanted his roads to be closed down, his opportunities taken away, and future relationships to be soured before they could even begin.

Now, as she was saying all this to me I was just listening. I was not only listening to her, but also to the voices of my spirits interjecting as she talked. As she was going on and on about how she was wronged, I could hear my spirits telling me how her motivation was not justified. My spirits were saying that this man did not wrong the client in such a way that deserved what she wanted. They were telling me that the client was actually upset because her control over him did not pan out as she expected, and she felt wronged because she lost what she per-ceived to be the upper hand and wanted him to pay. They were also very clear that the work was not work that should be done because it absolutely was not balanced.

So I asked the client if her ex-boyfriend had ever cheated on her. She said that he did not. I asked her if her ex-boyfriend ever abused her physically or mentally. She said that he never beat her, but did abuse her mentally. When I asked how, she said that he would yell at her when she kept after him about getting her way. She said that he sometimes addressed her with insulting words and that he called her selfish. I asked a few more probing questions to see where the issues were that would justify the work she requested. However, when she failed to provide that justification, I told her that I could not help her.

Needless to say, she got very upset. I simply told her that, based on what she had said were his grievous offenses and what my own spirits were saying, the work would not be balanced. I suggested that she just move forward with her life and focus on herself as opposed to the relationship that failed. She wasn't willing to hear that. She went to another worker who decided to take her case. The worker took her money and did the work but the work done against her ex-boyfriend came back on her. She lost her job, was in a car accident, and started seeing someone who stole from her.

This is a classic example of what will happen when work is not balanced. When the scales are tilted, it allows all sorts of chaos to come into your life and wreak havoc. Had she listened to my warning and the warning of my spirits, she would not have gone through what she did. Instead she had to learn the hard way. Be careful of roads that you close down or open up because if it is not something that keeps the scales in balance, it will open that door to chaos.

This is why the wisdom of our spirits and our ancestors is needed. They help us to see and discern how to proceed, both in our work and in our word. When you find it challenging to identify the balance of things, go to your ancestors. Their scope of vision is most likely broader than yours and their wisdom is invaluable when it comes to your work. The ancestors point to the path that you and your work should travel. Listen to them and avoid the foolishness that occurs when you don't.

Conjure work is a hard work. Conjure came about in this country to overcome oppression, to open doors, and to push back the slave drivers. A blessing and the turning of the other cheek would not have done the job. This might sound like I am pushing trick laying, but that is not the case. You must have both sides for the balance to be present.

Also in Conjure, there are a lot of folks who attempt to mold the work around what they want to do or around their other traditions. If you try and remove the root from a plant, what's going to happen? The plant will die. If you try and remove the root of a tradition, what's going to happen? The tradition loses its power and becomes about as potent as a wilted piece of lettuce.

Conjure is not Wicca. Conjure is not Buddhism. Conjure is not Hinduism. Conjure is not Satanism. Conjure is its own tradition with its own rules, and when you attempt to mold the tradition around another, you water it down until what you are doing is not Conjure. I am not saying that those other traditions aren't valuable. I am saying that Conjure does not bend to the likes or dislikes of the individual who is practicing it.

We are still living in times where oppression, deception, ill will, healing, cleansing, and both positive and negative opportunity play a part. Our ability to work what is necessary is something that is much needed, especially these days. For that reason, Conjure is alive and well, and we workers still have a part to play just as the work still has a part to play.

Do not be fearful of the other side of the coin because, sometimes, that other side of the coin is what's needed. On the same note, do not be the one to always lay a trick or a curse when wisdom is needed in both works. Instead, go to your ancestors. Listen to them. Seek the counsel of your spirits and learn to see the bigger picture. You might just find that your inhibitions no longer rule your work as much as they once did.

Embrace the work. Do the work. Be honorable and balanced. This is the calling card of any worker who possesses wisdom.

7

THE RIGHT AND LEFT HAND
OF CONJURE

The Right Hand work of Conjure is work that holds the power to bless, to heal, to open the roads, to bring prosperity, and so much more. Conjure was and still is very much driven toward survival and pushing forward.

The power of the root and the force of the ancestors drive the work and open the door for the magic to take hold and create the change in the proverbial tides. When we are sick, the work of Conjure makes us well.

When I was a kid and got sick, it was nothing to be put in a bathtub with a few caps full of ammonia and boiled bay leaves. I would have to wash myself while making prayers of healing and cleansing (usually Psalms 51 and 91). I didn't like those baths at all but, you know, they worked! I always felt better after and never stayed sick for long. Ammonia is something that has been used in Conjure for as long as I can remember. It is a cleanser of both spiritual and physical conditions alike. The ammonia and bay, combined with prayers and washing the sickness off, always opened the door for healing.

Conjure is very hands on, very practical, and very much a labor of the spirit. This work is not something you do only when the need arises. It is also done as part of daily routines. So, it is not something that you have to spend all sorts of time preparing for, but is rather a culture and a practice that come together. It is a mind-set of always being in the spirit while living in the physical and seeing both of those sides, day in and day out.

For example, every day, the house would get swept—starting in the back and moving toward the front. While sweeping, prayers of cleansing and protection are spoken. Petitions to the ancestors are also made so that the house is protected from evil and so it is not only cleansed physically, but also has the spiritual mud cleared away.

We would also make coffee for the ancestors. Why? The ancestors like coffee. Not only is coffee an offering to them, but also a cleanser. We give the coffee to the ancestors by putting it on their table and making prayers. After they finish with the coffee, we throw it out the front door. Some folks might think that is a bit odd, but the reason for it is to cleanse the steps of your house.

Taking offerings to the crossroads is another thing that should be done on a regular basis. Because the crossroads holds a very important part of what we do, it is common practice to drop some coins at the crossroads so that your roads stay open and your opportunities are always at your doorstep. You will find that just about every Conjure worker keeps a decent supply of coins in their car.

A wonderful part of the Right Hand of Conjure is that as we live our lives, not only in the practice of Conjure, but also in the culture of Conjure, we experience blessings on a daily basis that bring rewards on so many different levels. The work of Conjure keeps you blessed, clean, and walking the path of the crossroads no matter what adversity comes your way.

Conditions will always come and go. As they arise, we will answer the call to change them with our work, the work of Conjure.

I had a client a few years back who came to me because she had been subject to someone else's trick. She had been worked to the point that she was experiencing physical symptoms that would come and go. When the symptoms would come on she would feel sick, have pain in her stomach and lower back, and feel like she was in some sort of press. She had gone to the doctor to see what was wrong, but when the doctor did his exam and ran a few tests he couldn't find anything that could be causing it.

I asked her if she had any enemies who knew how to work. She explained that there was a woman she worked with who had been after her job for a long time. She said to me that she did not get along with this other woman and that about four months prior, they got into an argument that got pretty heated. It ended with the woman telling my client that she would be sorry for her disrespect.

I asked my client what the argument was about, and she explained that this woman would alter my client's paperwork to make it look like she made significant mistakes so she would look bad in front of her boss. My client decided she had enough of that and confronted the other woman, which is what sparked the argument.

The client told me that she didn't believe the woman knew how to work, but she thought the woman may have hired a worker to come after her. I asked her if the woman had taken anything of hers that she knew of. Things that could be linked to her—photos, hair, used eating utensils, and such. She didn't know, but regardless, she was experiencing pain that had no medical cause and wouldn't take care of itself.

So, I read on the condition and it looked like the other woman did have work done to my client. Reading on conditions is basically doing a divination to see what the nature of the circumstance or issue is. A condition is something going on that typically needs some sort of remedy. The reading or divination shows where the condition comes from and also what can be done to change it. From what I saw, it was as if my client had been nailed down under the foot of this other woman so that she could take her job.

So, I did a cleansing and some reversal work for this client. Reversal work (which some folks consider to be Left Handed) is when work is done to send other work back to where it came from. The cleansing that I did was seven baths that I made for her to take over seven days. The work in the baths was made to strip away the things that had been put on her. I also gave her instructions to put one cup of the bath water into a bottle after she finished each night. The reason for that is to use the tainted bath (the part that has all of the work that was washed off) against your enemy.

FIXING A CANDLE FOR REVERSAL AND SEPARATION

The reversal I did also included separation work.

Ingredients:

- 1 candle, plus 1 red pillar candle
- A glass of water
- Enough black wax to dip the red candle in about halfway

- A pot
- 1 pinch of sulphur
- 1 pinch of asafetida
- 1 pinch of valerian root
- A photo of the individual you are going to do the separation and reversal work on

Light your first candle and offer it to the four directions and put a glass of water down.

Next put the black wax in a pot and begin to melt it.

While you are melting the wax, add in the roots.

You also take the photo and burn it into ash and add that to the black wax as well.

Once that is done, take a red candle and dip it in the black wax, making a two-colored candle.

∞∞∞∞

Once the candle was fixed, I had the client rub herself down with it, making her prayers and petitions against the enemy. She rubbed the candle over the areas where the pain was located, over her hands, as well as her legs and feet.

After that was done, I took the candle and made my own declarations against the enemy of the client—for the work done against my client to be undone, for the two of them to be separated, and for the return of everything that had been done. Sometimes you just have to put that stamp "return to sender" on some work and let them have it back.

I burned the candle for her for one hour each day for three days, making prayers and petitions over it so that the work would be undone on my client and sent back to the one who started it.

Now, remember how I said that I had my client take a cup of the used bath each day and put it into a bottle? Let's get back to that. The used bath carries in it the essences of what was done to my client. The washing strips it off and taints the water with it. So, if you take some of that water and go to the house of your enemy, you can pour it onto the front door area of their house. When they step in it, guess what? They get exactly what they gave.

My client did that very thing. After the work was finished, the baths taken, and the tainted water poured on the other woman's doorstep, things changed. My client no longer had the pain where she felt like someone was stomping on her. The other woman experienced a separation from my client by way of getting fired from her job. Apparently, it came to light that she was purposefully and maliciously creating paperwork errors and she was terminated for that. Also, the pain that my client had experienced, the other woman began to experience. My client said to me that the woman was in pain and described it almost identically to what she had experienced when the work was done to her. All of this work took ten days to manifest. But it was ten days of steady and consistent work that overcame the enemy and brought cleansing and healing, as well as the separation needed to end the continually stressful negative situation.

ooooo

Folks often confuse the Left Hand of Conjure, including justice, tricks, vengeance, and overcoming various types of oppression, with being evil, immoral, or just plain wrong. As you can see from the last example, that isn't the case. Just because it makes some folks uncomfortable does not mean that it does not have its place. Take the weather for example. Beautiful sunny days are great, but the storm has its place here as well. It is the storm that stirs everything up and moves things around. It also gives water to the plants, without which they would die. When we work in Conjure we need both, because it is both that keeps things in balance.

Conjure's Left Hand is one that comes with its own responsibilities, of course. I am not advising you to just go around and tie up or curse everything that moves. There must be balance. If the work calls for it, then do it. Just like with the example I gave in chapter 6 of someone breaking into your house, if there is a threat, the work calls for ensuring the threat is stopped. Once the threat has been squashed, you can resume what you were doing before.

Conjure is not about turning the other cheek. The theory of karma or the Three-Fold Law is not part of Conjure. Conjure is about keeping things in balance, making magical change using spiritual work that reflects from the world of the spirit back into the world of the physical. It is about the principle of the crossroads, where the the physical and the spirit intersect, and there is a reflection of one into the other. At the crossroads, each of them has the ability to manifest into the other. A very simple example would be to fix a candle and make prayers for money. The next day you find some money on the ground, get a raise at work, or are given money that may be owed to you. The work of the spirit was done and it manifested into the physical.

I had someone who came to me for a consultation some years back. This person had been the victim of an abusive family relationship. The object of both physical and mental abuse from his father, my client had lived most of his life in fear of the man who constantly told that he was nothing, no good, and should have been drowned when was born. He would receive weekly beatings, where he was hit in the face with both open hands and closed fists. He was made to eat things that were disgusting and would be beaten if he didn't. When he was old enough, he left his house and moved out on his own. Even though he left that house, his father continued to harass and stalk him. Although the physical abuse stopped, the mental and verbal abuse was still very present and had a strong effect on him. It was difficult for him to keep a job, he didn't sleep well, and he had internalized the abuse. His self-image was so low he truly believed he was no good.

I initially met him at a coffee shop. He was standing in front of me in line. I noticed that he was a bit jittery and had this odd look on his face, as if the sky was about to fall. I had to ask him if he was okay. He blurted out that he was okay, but that someone was after him. That struck me as a bit odd, so I asked him if he wanted to have coffee with me. He agreed.

After hearing all of the things he was subjected to through his life and was continuing to experience, my heart went out to him. The things he went through no one should have to endure. He had said that he prayed often for his situation to change, but that nothing ever happened. He even told me that he didn't believe in anything because, if God existed, he wouldn't have let him stay in such a horrible situation.

I told him that sometimes things happen that aren't so good, but that doesn't mean they cannot be corrected. I also told him that I was a Conjure man and I did spiritual work that could change things up. He only halfheartedly believed me, but I didn't really care. All I wanted to do was help him and he agreed that he needed it. This unbalanced business needed to be brought back to balance and some justice work was just the thing.

I went to my spirits, my ancestors, and told them what had gone on with this client and asked for their aid and intervention with him. I told them that his father was still, in his own sick way, stalking him and keeping him mentally bound and unable to move forward. They said they would help.

I obtained the name of his father and managed to get some other things I needed from the client including his father's address, which was nearby. I had decided that it was time to cross him up and turn those tables. I made some crossing powder and fixed a black candle with some Black Arts oil.

Crossing powder is an amazing thing that can be used to shut down the crossroads on someone. It also brings bad luck and opens the doors for all sorts of not-so-good things to happen. Black Arts oil is good for attracting malevolent spirits that delight in making misery and chaos. Those spirits are almost parasitic because they will literally feed on those they go after.

So, after the crossing powder was finished, I took it to my client's father's house, at around four in the morning. Yes, in Conjure, sometimes we have to be like ninjas and move in the shadows. I laid the trick at his front door and also put some on the door handle of his car. You see, with these powders, physical contact is primarily how the trick is laid and activated. So, if you spray some hair spray on a door handle, for example, you can sprinkle the powder on it and it will stick.

After the powder was laid at the door, the following night, I fixed the candle with the Black Arts oil and put him in the candle. To do that you take some link to the person (name paper, hair, unwashed clothing, and such) and add it to the candle itself. You can take a photo, for example, and burn it into ash and rub it into the candle. You could also take some hair and melt some wax off the side of the candle to put it in. Then reseal the candle with the wax you melted off.

The candle work was done each night for one hour over a nine-day period. A lot of the time we work in cycles. Since the Black Arts work is associated with malevolent dead spirits and the number nine is often associated with the dead, we do it for nine days. Once the ninth day was done, I took the wax that was left to the graveyard and buried it at the central crossroads located there.

I contacted the client and told him that I had finished the work and that things were about to go down. He said he was being harassed, that his father had called him, drunk, and was telling him that he would never amount to anything more than the "piece of shit he was born to be." I told him not to worry, the trick had been laid and it was going to kick in.

About a week and a half later, my client called me and told me that his father had been thrown in jail. I asked what happened. He said that his father was at a bar that he frequented and got into a fight. Apparently, he broke a bottle over someone's head at the bar and then left. The bar called the police and they found him driving toward his house. The police pulled him over and arrested him. They charged him with aggravated battery and DUI. Needless to say, he was going to be in jail for a long time and would not be able to stalk or abuse my client anymore. My client was very happy about that.

I met him back at the same coffee shop and we talked. He had this look of relief on his face and his spirit was not as down in the dumps anymore. Granted, he still had a lot of work to undo all of his father's negative conditioning, but he was definitely on the road to healing, cleansing, and getting himself lifted up.

Conjure came about as a way to overcome oppression and that is exactly what this client was experiencing. This was a case where the Left Hand of Conjure was absolutely necessary. Things were unbalanced and needed to be brought back into balance. So, when you look at Conjure, if you look at it in a way that isn't about good and evil, but about balance, you will see things differently. The left side is not one to shun or be fearful of, but is a part of the way Conjure works. Remember, there are two sides to the coin and both are essential.

When you grasp the principle that the work is the work and the balance of both sides is very important in the bigger picture, you will truly be able to add potency there. Not only in your work, but also in how you live, day to day. Things are not always meant to be nice nor are they meant to be pretty. It is up to you to make that decision; however, if you are going to be working Conjure, then you must remember how the roots of Conjure were built. Don't rip out the foundation of the house if you don't want it to fall.

8

THE SPIRIT OF PLACE

The work of Conjure/Hoodoo is very practical and involves performing actual labors in order to change the condition of whatever the circumstances might be. Conjure is not a religion, but a tradition of work that holds strong ties with the spirits of the root, God, and the ancestors.

Another strong tie that Conjure has is to what we would call the *spirit of place*. The spirit of place is something that holds potent power, based on a physical location. We often hear about different spaces that have potency, such as the crossroads or the graveyard, but there is so much more when it comes to these different areas. In this chapter, I am going to go into more detail about different spirits of place. Much like earlier, when I was talking about the power of the dirts and how different physical places hold power based on what has been established and worked there (page 47), I am now going to go over places that hold spiritual potency and the work that is done there. These places are physical places that have essences in them of spiritual force and spiritual power.

The spirit of place can actually mean a couple of things. It can mean that there has been so much of a specific type of work done there that a spiritual resonance with a certain kind of work has been established over time. It can also mean that there are spirits who dwell in certain areas that are not against giving assistance or aid when to comes to the work the Conjure man or Conjure woman is doing.

For example, when there is a place where one or more workers go to do cleansing work, over time, that place becomes a power point where cleansing is done. The spirits that live there and the earth itself will begin to lend themselves to that type of work. If you have an altar where you do all of your work, how does it feel compared to the rest of the house? Is there a different feeling when you go to it that lets you know that work is about to begin? Does the altar have that spirit of work present, as opposed to, say, the relaxed spirit of the living room? I would daresay it does and it is this principle that may best describe establishing working relationships with various spirits of place.

Let's talk about a few of the spirits of place, then.

The Crossroads

I love the crossroads and most of the spirits that live there. The crossroads is that intersection where the world of the physical and the world of the spirit come together. The crossroads is, both physically and spiritually, just as it looks, a place that both the spirits and folks with bodies travel through. It opens the doors of opportunity as well as shuts them. The crossroads always presents itself in such a way that there is a choice to be made.

When it comes to the work of the crossroads, there are many things that can be done there, but the spirit of the place of the crossroads is one that gives opportunity or takes it away. The place of the crossroads can be used to open doors for someone or to shut them down and make that person wish he had never wronged a worker or her client. But it's the blessing of creating opportunity where there may not have been one that is one of the most potent aspects of this truly powerful place.

The River

The spirit of the river also gives and takes away. Rivers are among those places where you can remove bad work and perform powerful cleansings, such as renewal of the soul. You can even take away the foolishness that has become a plague on your own life.

The river brings life itself. Its waters feed the areas it flows through. The river carries boats that bring trade to ports that sustain the folks who live there. The river brings prosperity. Baptism traditionally occurred in the river because the water needed to be moving and cold, so that the spirit of the person being baptized not only is cleansed, but also the old part of them is actually washed away. When I speak of the river, I am including other flowing bodies of fresh water such as creeks, as they have a similar spirit.

The Ocean

The ocean is one of the most mysterious and majestic places in this world to me. It has such a strength and potency that I always take notice. The ocean is powerful when it comes to works of creation. The water, deep and wide, is just like a womb that has the potential to give birth. There are also very strong healing qualities there. Like the river, the ocean both gives and takes away. It is the power of the ocean that can provide fish to the fisherman and it is also the power of the ocean that can create a tidal wave that will wipe out an entire town.

The Railroad

The iron on the tracks, the power of the train, the sweat of the brow of those who came before us and laid those tracks bring us to a very strong place where protection, travel, and the fortitude to overcome join together. The railroad is a perfect place to do work for fortification, force, and the power to be victorious over enemies as well as circumstances. The spikes of the railroad are very potent for protection, and the spirit of that place is one where you can literally feel power emanating from it.

The Woods

In the woods there are many secrets. It is a place where you find growth, life, death, blessing, and even cursing. The spirit of the woods is one that I would say holds a lot of mystery, but it is also a place that is, literally, filled with the power of the earth. I have worked both blessings and curses, cleansings and prosperity, as well as separation and drawing in love there. I love to go into the woods because, much like the ocean, you never know what you will find.

The Mountain

The spirit of the mountain always has a feeling of old work for me. The mountain is strong and able to withstand even the most difficult of storms. Coming from the mountains, I always notice how old the spirits feel there. The interesting part about it is that in some places you could feel the desire to work, while in other places, the mountain couldn't care less about what you were doing. The mountain is a very good place for foundational work and works of strength and fortitude. It also holds a potent spirit of protection. The mountain is also a place of seriousness. You won't find much playfulness there.

The Graveyard

The graveyard is one of the most interesting places we will talk about. The power of the graveyard has many facets to it and the spirit of place that dwells there can be very different, depending on the graveyard. Some are sleepy while others are wide awake. On one hand you can go there to do amazingly terrible curse work, and on the other hand you can go to do work that has the power of the dead fueling great blessings. The graveyard is a place where it is absolutely vital that you establish a working relationship before you attempt to do any spiritual work. It can be extremely volatile, but can also be one of the most humbling and rewarding places you will have the privilege to work.

The Place of New Orleans

The spirit of place is one that, very much, includes geographic locations as well and I would be remiss if I didn't talk about my home in New Orleans.

New Orleans has a very strong spirit of place. It is a city that is truly built on the dead and where the spirits are very much awake and speak. In New Orleans the dead are everywhere, not just in the graveyards. In fact, they have been found buried under the French Quarter, among other places. There was a story that came out about a bunch of coffins discovered around the corner of Rampart Street and Burgundy Street (Buh-gun-dee, is how we say it in New Orleans). As it turns out, it was an old graveyard that was built over as the French Quarter expanded. It is actually older than the famed St. Louis Cemetary No. 1. However, that is not something that is uncommon. There are bones and people everywhere here.

And so, we are also called, at times, a city of the dead. Mainly because the graveyards are all above ground. The fact that city was built in a swamp makes it a bit challenging to keep the dead in the ground. The point is you can walk down the street and literally hear spirits talking. It is not uncommon to hear footsteps of spirits following you around or to even see them looking at you. New Orleans has many spirits that have come together to create what the city is. The spiritual potency runs very thick here.

There is also a not-so-good side of the spirit of place here. Folks often ask me about New Orleans and express their desire to move here. I tell them that there is a tremendous freedom here, both in the physical and spiritual worlds that have the ability to draw out fleshly attributes. For example, some of the spirits around here facilitate temptation that could bring any potential vice you might have to the surface. If you have a predisposition to drug addiction, alcoholism, or sex addiction, some of those spirits will certainly try to coax it out.

You will often hear that New Orleans either welcomes you or will spit you out. This is one of the truest statements about the spirit of this place that could be made. To be in the middle of the power that is so thick in this city requires strength and will.

Can you do powerful work here? Yes indamndeed, you can. Can you be overcome here? Yes indamndeed, you can.

ooooo

The spirit of place is something that folks need to begin to feel out, in order to understand its potential. This potential is a powerful tool that can be used for spiritual work as well as in everyday life. However, you must take the time to understand each spirit's various strengths and weaknesses. It is in that understanding that you can tap into your own wisdom and do what you need to do for yourself or somebody else.

9

CONJURE IN THE GRAVEYARD

I am starting this chapter off with one of my favorite biblical passages because the principles of the graveyard are highly connected with the relationship between the worker and the spirits. It comes from Ezekiel chapter 37:1–14:

37 THE HAND OF THE LORD WAS UPON ME, AND CARRIED ME OUT IN THE SPIRIT OF THE LORD, AND SET ME DOWN IN THE MIDST OF THE VALLEY WHICH WAS FULL OF BONES,

2 AND CAUSED ME TO PASS BY THEM ROUND ABOUT: AND, BEHOLD, THERE WERE VERY MANY IN THE OPEN VALLEY; AND, LO, THEY WERE VERY DRY.

3 AND HE SAID UNTO ME, SON OF MAN, CAN THESE BONES LIVE? AND I ANSWERED, O LORD GOD, THOU KNOWEST.

4 AGAIN HE SAID UNTO ME, PROPHESY UPON THESE BONES, AND SAY UNTO THEM, O YE DRY BONES, HEAR THE WORD OF THE LORD.

5 Thus saith the Lord God unto these bones;
Behold, I will cause breath to enter into you, and
ye shall live:

6 And I will lay sinews upon you, and will bring up
flesh upon you, and cover you with skin, and put
breath in you, and ye shall live; and ye shall know
that I am the Lord.

7 So I prophesied as I was commanded: and as I
prophesied, there was a noise, and behold a shaking, and the bones came together, bone to his
bone.

8 And when I beheld, lo, the sinews and the flesh
came up upon them, and the skin covered them
above: but there was no breath in them.

9 Then said he unto me, Prophesy unto the wind,
prophesy, son of man, and say to the wind, Thus
saith the Lord God; Come from the four winds, O
breath, and breathe upon these slain, that they
may live.

10 So I prophesied as he commanded me, and the
breath came into them, and they lived, and stood
up upon their feet, an exceeding great army.

11 Then he said unto me, Son of man, these bones
are the whole house of Israel: behold, they say,
Our bones are dried, and our hope is lost: we are
cut off for our parts.

12 Therefore prophesy and say unto them, Thus
saith the Lord God; Behold, O my people, I will
open your graves, and cause you to come up out of
your graves, and bring you into the land of Israel.

13 AND YE SHALL KNOW THAT I AM THE LORD, WHEN I
HAVE OPENED YOUR GRAVES, O MY PEOPLE, AND BROUGHT
YOU UP OUT OF YOUR GRAVES,

14 AND SHALL PUT MY SPIRIT IN YOU, AND YE SHALL
LIVE, AND I SHALL PLACE YOU IN YOUR OWN LAND: THEN
SHALL YE KNOW THAT I THE LORD HAVE SPOKEN IT, AND
PERFORMED IT, SAITH THE LORD.

People have differing opinions about the cemetery. Some say that it is a place of rest, some say it is a place of work, and others say that it is a place of communion with the dead. I happen to agree with all of these opinions

In the world there are many places that hold a lot of power, for example, the crossroads and the river. The graveyard is also one of those places. It is a place that has been consecrated with prayers and blessings so that the dead can be at peace and the spirits can have their rest, should they so choose. See, the dead are always talking, but sometimes we may not be able to hear them because of blocks, because of not maintaining relationships with those spirits, or whatever the reason may be. It is my goal in this chapter to show you how to effectively work in the graveyard and experience the raw power of the dead themselves—or better yet, allow them to show you.

When you hold a desire to work with spirits, specifically the dead, there are things you must take note of first. Trust and believe that you aren't going to just walk into the graveyard and every spirit living there is going to throw themselves at you. The dead, much like those with bodies, can be fickle and have the ability to make their own choices about who they work with or what they will do.

To put it simply, you have to begin with the legwork. That includes regular visits to the graveyard, coming around so they can see you, and talking to them. So, let's begin with how to go in and out of the graveyard.

Coming In and Out of the Graveyard

Entering the graveyard in a lot of ways is like going to someone's house. You never go empty-handed. Offerings for the entrance of the graveyard are necessary. Think of it as a friendly way to say to the gatekeeper that you are there and you brought gifts. Offerings can include things like coins, candy, whiskey, rum, cigarettes, and cigars. The dead like those things and they will provide a better welcome than if you just waltz in empty-handed.

Also, when you go to the graveyard, you should always have your head covered. Protection is always a must when you are dealing with gathering places of spirits. Not every spirit in the graveyard is going to like you and there are others that may try to attach themselves to you so they can follow you home. Covering your head is good protection, and when it is followed with a cleansing, it is a good practice for keeping things off you that don't need to be there.

After you make your offerings at the gate of the graveyard, you can go ahead and go in. Now, there are folks who will hide their faces when they enter and exit the graveyard because some spirits can have strong working relationships with other workers and you wouldn't want them to be telling your business, would you? Some folks will put their hands over their face when they cross the threshold of the graveyard and some folks will enter it backward. That, of course is up to you. However, I can tell you that I never just walk into the graveyard and show my face as I cross the gate. There was a worker I knew a long time ago who would put a handkerchief over her face when she walked into the graveyard. She wasn't taking any chances! This is primarily applicable to doing work or giving offerings to the dead you work with in the graveyard. I am not saying that if you are going to a funeral you need to do this, but the point I am making is that you don't want to be exposed in your work by another worker who might want to mess with it. Workers are always cautious and cunning in every aspect of the work they do. This is no exception.

ooooo

When it is time to leave the graveyard, you will want to follow similar protocols as when you entered. When you are doing work in the graveyard, after it is complete and you are ready to go, you typically do not look back at it. There are a couple of reasons for this. Looking back at it can be a sign of a lack of faith in the work, worry, or an uncertainty about what was done. If you are going to do work, then you need to be confident in it. This is not to say that by doing that you are exhibiting any of those feelings, however an outward sign can often reveal an inner feeling. Another reason I have talked about before is that there can be spirits in the graveyard who have a working relationship with another spiritual worker. If that is the case, when they go to examine the work you did, they may very well report it back to the worker they have that kind of bond with. I don't know about you, but when it comes to my work I do not want anyone messing with it or giving it an opportunity to be undone.

Once you are exiting the graveyard, you do not need to leave offerings as you did when you came in. When you are leaving someone's house you don't tend to give gifts at that time. Gifts are most often given when you are arriving. The same principle applies here. However, just as you would thank your host when you are getting ready to go, you would also give a word or two of gratitude to the spirits of the graveyard. Having some manners with the spirits of the dead, just as you would with those in life, will open the door for better working relationships and more willingness to do the things that are asked of them. I know that if someone were to be courteous and have home training when they need me to do something, I would be more apt to help them. If, however, they were discourteous and rude, well, then they get it how they live (which means I am not going to lift a damn finger to help).

Forming a Working Relationship with Spirits of the Graveyard

When you are a spiritual worker, you will always have relationships with spirits. It sounds so simple to say, but some folks may not completely understand the concept of relationships with spirits. We have our ancestors, who are the most important spirits we can have around us. It is our ancestors that are our biggest allies and who hold so much wisdom that not only strengthens our work, but also brings growth so that we may continue to blaze the trail that they once did. Relationships with them are always the most important but you can also develop relationships with other spirits that have a strong place in your work and its potency and growth.

The spirits of the graveyard, as I have said before, are both positive and negative, just as people are in life. Some may want to work with you while others do not. To begin this process, yes, it is a process, you begin by finding someone who lives there to ask.

Go and have a visit in the graveyard and see if you feel a pull to anyone. A lot of the time, there are spirits that will take notice of you and, perhaps, want to come to you and begin a working relationship. It can be someone who has been forgotten, someone who has not been lifted up by her own folks, or even someone who is simply hungry. Yes, even the dead get hungry.

Bring with you some offerings, as always, and walk around the place. While you are doing that, be aware of what is going on around you. The dead are always speaking, but sometimes we don't hear them, so it is important that you are listening, watching, and feeling what is going on around you. When you get the sense that someone is trying to tell you something, find out who it is. Look at the gravestone and see who is there. Now, I would do a little research to see about this person. Perhaps you could find out who they were, how they died, and what kind of life they lived. Most importantly, you need to trust your gut. If you feel comfort and happiness or contentment, then chances are the formation of a working relationship is a good thing. If those feelings are a bit of dread, fear, or malice, you might want to leave them alone. Either way, you need to pay attention to those feelings because your own spirits and your own discernment will lead you in the right direction.

Once you have found your new acquaintance, sit with her and begin a conversation. I can hear folks now, saying, "That's it?" In the beginning, yes, that's it. Just like when you make a new friend, you don't immediately start planning to go on vacations together. You get to know one another and start building connections.

Also, you will want to give her offerings and such, as a sign of good faith, as well as some edification when it comes to building a relationship. Flowers are good, as are liquor and food. Giving these offerings does a couple of things. They are an act of respect for the spirit. It also keeps things balanced and shows that you are not just trying to take and take. Offerings are also sources of sustenance for those spirits. As I've said before, even the dead have to eat. Giving them offerings makes them stronger and also makes them more inclined to work with you.

Make it a regular thing to go and visit whoever it is that you are forming a working relationship with. Being consistent will strengthen the bond and open the door to having an ally in the graveyard who is willing to do work with you. Do not expect to go to the graveyard once and instantaneously become a spirit whisperer. This work takes time to develop and so do the relationships that are established. You should go and see her at least once a week and talk. As you are talking to her you can ask her to reveal more of herself to you. Ask her what she would like as offerings. Each spirit has her own tastes, so it is good to know what she likes. When you give her things she likes, not only does it make her happy and more inclined to be around you, but also confirms that you are hearing the voice of that spirit.

How do you know what she likes? Again, ask her. You may hear or feel that she want donuts and vodka or something like that. Well, go get some donuts and vodka and give it to her and see if you heard her right. If she likes it, you will know. If she doesn't, you will know.

As you spend more time with her and that relationship develops, your own sensitivity to the spirit increases as well. That is very important because when we are sensitive to the spirit we have another voice that brings direction, confirmation, and wisdom not just in our work but also in our daily lives. It also doesn't hurt to have more spirits at your side!

After some time has passed and you have been consistent in spending time with that spirit of the graveyard, now it would be time to begin to ask her about doing a work with you. You are going to begin with simple things, like a protection or a simple blessing. The work grows as you grow with that spirit. If you are learning to shoot a gun, you probably aren't gonna start out by firing a missile. Same thing applies here. Exercising and building the relationship is something that requires time but brings potency to your work and opens doors to the spiritual path you are walking.

The Importance of Cleansing after You Leave the Graveyard

Cleansing is such an important part of the work that I cannot stress it enough—especially when you are working in the graveyard. As I have said before, not all spirits in the graveyard are friendly or have the best intentions. There are spirits that live there who are looking for a free meal, who can be tricky and deceptive. This is one of the main reasons why, first and foremost, you must be protected when you are in the graveyard. There are some spirits that can be a bit parasitic in that they want to attach themselves to you and syphon off your energy. That is why, when you leave the graveyard you need to make it a specific requirement to do a cleansing. You don't want to take anything home with you that turns into an issue later. If you do not practice regular spiritual cleansing then I can guarantee that there will come a time when you don't leave alone.

Places you go, people you visit, things you see and feel all have their place, but being vigilant in keeping yourself cleansed in all these things will only serve to improve your life and stop foolishness before it begins. The graveyard is no exception to this, and is, in fact, one of the more volatile places where this principle must be upheld.

When you are in the graveyard, especially one where other workers have things going on, you also have to keep in mind that other work can spill over onto you. It may not be meant for you, but depending on the skill, or lack thereof, of the other workers, it absolutely can have effects on you. For example, if you were to step in or on someone else's work, that work can attach itself to you, giving you even more to contend with.

I know someone who walked into one of the graveyards here in New Orleans a little while back. This person was going into the graveyard to do some work for a client. Specifically, going to the dead to remove someone out of their client's life. While in the graveyard, there was a doll baby that was lying next to one of the gravestones. He didn't see it and accidentally stepped on it. He told me that the doll baby looked as if it had been there a while, had some nails in its head and some faded petition that was pinned to it. He couldn't make out what was on the petition, but he put the doll baby back where it was before he disturbed it.

He did the work he was there to do and then left the graveyard. The next day, he began to experience sickness that came out of nowhere. He was having migraine headaches and throwing up for no apparent reason. He didn't know what was going on so he called me and told me what had happened. I asked him if he had taken a cleansing bath after leaving the graveyard. For one, he was doing work in the graveyard, and secondly, he had disturbed (unwittingly, but disturbed nonetheless) someone else's work and God knows what kind of work it was. He said that he had not done the cleansing after and was now feeling as if he were being kicked in the stomach and being hit in the head by a hammer.

I went to his house and gave him a cleansing bath, made some prayers, and wrapped up his head. The following day the pain was gone and it was as if nothing happened. See, when you are doing work, you must not only be very aware of your surroundings, but also make sure that you follow through with the aftercare. If he had done the cleansing after, then the work wouldn't have set in on him.

A QUICK CLEANSING FOR AFTER THE GRAVEYARD

When you leave the graveyard, you should have something on hand to start the cleansing process. It can keep the work of the graveyard off of you until you get home to do the cleansing bath. When you go to places where things are tainted you can become tainted, hence the importance of washing it off.

Ingredients:

- Salt—a potent cleanser to send away the dead
- Florida Water—another very good cleanser

Simply take a few pinches of salt in the palm of your hand. Pour some Florida Water on your palm with the salt in it. Rub the two together and put it on the forehead, the back of the neck, the heart, the hands, and the feet. Doing this is a surface cleansing until a stronger one can be done when you get home. It is as simple as keeping a bit of salt and a bottle of Florida Water in your car and using it once you exit the graveyard. You can also use these ingredients for a bath.

When you leave the graveyard, you should have some of this on hand to start that cleansing process. When you are doing a cleansing on yourself, you need to make sure you are washing from the head downward, pushing off the foolishness that doesn't need to be there. Take the mixture and put some on the places where spirits and work can adhere to you and that should be handled immediately:

- Your head—the place of knowledge

- Your neck—an entry point for spirits

- Your heart—the place of sensitivity

- Your hands—the place of work

- Your feet—the place that enables you to walk your path accordingly

On a side note, I am of the opinion that cleansings should *not* be done in the graveyard. Some may disagree with me and that's okay, but I would be remiss if I did not express this and why.

As a worker, I would never, ever take someone into the graveyard to do a cleansing. When you perform a cleansing on someone, it's like giving them new, tender skin. The old things are torn off, the foolishness is removed, and they are new again.

Now, if you were a parasite and you saw someone who was tender and easy to attach yourself to, would you? Just like babies who don't have developed immune systems, they must be cared for carefully.

The same principle applies here. If you cleanse someone in the graveyard, the parasitic spirits that dwell there can easily attach themselves to the newly cleansed individual and wreak havoc. Some folks will say that they are skilled and have secrets for effective cleansing in the graveyard. Perhaps they do, but why risk it when you don't have to? I have personally seen graveyard cleansings do the opposite. Part of it may have been due to the lack of skill or wisdom of the worker who did it, but at the same time, the graveyard is not a place of cleansing. The reason I add this here is that I was contacted by someone who had some not-so-great results after a cleansing he received in the graveyard.

This individual had contacted a worker and asked for a spiritual cleansing. The worker took him to one of the graveyards and performed the spiritual cleansing on him. After it was done, my client was advised to just leave some offerings for the spirits there. He was given no aftercare instructions, no direction in what should be done moving forward, none of that. Well, once the cleansing was done, things did not go so well for him. Within the span of one week, he lost his job, lost his relationship, was in a car accident, and was arrested on some bogus charge. Now, I don't know about you, but if all that foolishness is going on directly after receiving this great and powerful cleansing in the graveyard, I would certainly wonder what happened once it was done.

In this work, we do not play dress up or pretend. We take what we do seriously and have the responsibility to care for those who come to us for help. This sheer lack of wisdom on the part of that worker created utter chaos for the client he was charged with performing work for. Spiritual work is no joke and should never be done willy-nilly. Personally, it was my opinion he took the client into the graveyard so he could appear to be spooky or powerful, but at the end of the day his client paid the price for it. When all is said and done, you have the responsibility of doing your work and doing it well. Anything else is absolutely unacceptable.

A CLEANSING BATH FOR AFTER THE GRAVEYARD

A very good bath for cleansing after you leave the graveyard uses two large pinches of salt, three large pinches of hyssop, three large pinches of rue, and some Florida Water.

The Graveyard as a Place of Power

The graveyard holds within it a power that is both positive and negative, kind and angry, uplifting and tearing down. Its volatile nature makes it, in my opinion, one of the most potent places in existence. Inside the graveyard you have spirits of the dead who have varied intentions as well as varied interests. Some spirits of the graveyard have no problem working with someone to tear down an enemy while others have no issue with offering their assistance to bring protection to the Conjure man or woman.

Even the ground itself is full of differing types of power. From the grave of someone who was murdered to the grave of someone who spent their life protecting others, these essences become part of the place itself. Learning to navigate this potent place takes time and can be tricky even for experienced workers, however, we do what we do and continue to do the work.

The interesting thing about the dead and the graveyard is that there is a tremendous amount of wisdom there. Spirits of the dead hold the wisdom of their own lives, wisdom they have gained since they left their bodies, and wisdom of their own observations in dealing with other spirits of the dead.

When we work in the graveyard we have to keep in mind that it is a place where new knowledge can be acquired, new relationships can be formed, and honing our skill as a worker is something that can absolutely be manifested. The power of the graveyard can build up and tear down. There are always two sides of the coin, and the graveyard exhibits both of these qualities.

The power that resides in the graveyard comes from the spirits that live there—those who have passed and become residents of that place. All of those experiences from all of those people coming together in one place creates a potency of the spirit that has its own rules and its own personality. When you stand in the middle of the graveyard and can feel the eyes of those spirits looking back at you, you begin to take notice of the place and the ones who live there.

Personally, I find the graveyard to be one of the most potent places for work. The graveyard and the crossroads have what

I would call their own spiritual highways that can be tapped into to do a lot of work and to do it well. This isn't to say that other places are not potent; that would be foolish. Speaking for myself, I tend to like the dead and am always looking to hear the latest wisdom they have to offer. Standing in the graveyard is like feeling the heartbeat of the spirits themselves.

A MOJO HAND FOR PROSPERITY IN THE GRAVEYARD

Prosperity is something that, in one way or another, we all strive for. We like the idea of continuous financial blessings, the ability to pay our way, and having our needs met. Here is a work you can do in the graveyard to help that very thing manifest.

Ingredients:

- A few pinches of orange peel—to attract prosperity and money
- 7 black-eyed peas—for luck and open roads
- A small piece of ginger root (*Zingiber officinale*)—to heat the work and draw to you
- A few silver coins, plus a few more coins for offering
- A clipping of your dominant hand's index fingernail—to draw money and assign the bag to you
- A small cloth bag
- A trowel
- Some rum or whiskey

Now, before you do any of this, you should establish a relationship with a banker or businessperson in the graveyard. To begin to build a relationship with one of the dead there are several things you need to do. First, you need to be a regular visitor in the graveyard. If you are seen by the dead on a consistent basis, they tend to open up. Next, you will need to find a banker or businessperson and begin to talk with them. Talking and listening are very important in this work. It helps to build a rapport. Also, be sure to bring offerings—things like coins, food, drinks, and various items like that. The building of a working relationship with a spirit takes time and effort. The more work you put in, the more the spirits will be willing to work with you. Once you have established that relationship, you are going to ask for their help in the work.

After the spirit agrees to help, you can begin the rest of the work. Start by giving light and water as well as offerings to the roots. Also make your petitions and prayers over them.

Once you have done that, you are going to put the roots, along with the silver coins and the fingernail clipping, in the bag.

Take the filled bag to the graveyard and to the spirit that agreed to help you. You are going to dig a small hole at their grave. When you dig the hole, pour in a bit of rum or whiskey and put in offering coins. Once you have put them in the hole, you can place the bag that will become the hand inside. Make your prayers and petitions for prosperity, and ask the spirit that lives there to give his assistance in the work and to add to its potency.

Then you are going to bury the hand in the hole and pour a little more rum or whiskey on top.

You will leave the hand there for seven days. After the seventh day you will come back and dig it up. When you dig up the hand, you will, again, put offerings there, giving thanks for the work and to the spirit that helped.

Once you have finished, you will carry the hand in your pocket to draw prosperity to yourself. What you have done is created a mojo hand that is also infused with the power of the dead—in this case, the power of someone who, in life, was successful in the area of prosperity. This adds to the power of the hand because it gives it an additional platform for drawing that very thing to you. If you are right-handed, you should carry the hand in your left pocket and vice versa if you are left-handed because, as I was taught, your nondominant hand draws work to you and your dominant hand sends it out.

A WORK AGAINST AN ENEMY IN THE GRAVEYARD

I spent some time talking about one side of the coin in the graveyard, so I would be remiss if I didn't give you a work on the other side of that coin. It is about balance after all.

For this work, you are going to be making a doll baby for your enemy. The doll baby is a potent form of work that can be used for both the positive and the negative. I am not going to tell you to make a doll and start sticking pins in it; that is for someone else. What I will tell you is that the doll baby can be quite effective in all sorts of work dealing with specific people.

ooooo

Ingredients:

- A glass of water

- A black candle

- Some Spanish moss (*Tillandsia usneoides*)—to form the doll baby; good for laying tricks, binding up, and the like

- A few twigs (optional)—to form the skeleton

- Something personal of your enemy (photograph, hair, nail clippings, etc.)

- Spray adhesive or hairspray—to make the sulphur stick

- Some sulphur powder—to draw malevolent spirits
- Some guinea peppers (*Aframomum melegueta*)—to heat the work
- Some black cloth—to wrap the doll baby
- Some holy water—to connect the doll baby and the enemy
- A covering for your head
- A few coins
- Some rum or whiskey
- Some twine

When you have everything together, get a glass of water and light a black candle. This work should be done during the transition from day to night. When you are working with the dead the best time to do so is after the sun is gone. This is not to say it cannot be done in the day, but the night offers more effective graveyard work because those spirits are more active.

Now you can begin to form the body of your doll baby using the Spanish moss. While you are doing so, you are going to be speaking directly against your enemy—cursing them, their name, and anything else you want to declare.

Once the body is formed, you are going to add your enemy's personal items to the body of the doll baby.

When you have done that, you can spray the doll baby with some adhesive, hairspray, or something along those lines. When you have sprayed the body of the doll baby, you can sprinkle the sulphur powder on it. You want to do that while the spray is still damp so it gets a good stick to it and the powder doesn't go everywhere.

You are also going to put your guinea peppers in the doll baby—some in the head and some in the heart area will be just fine. The spray adhesive or hairspray should hold it in place. If you are afraid that the guinea peppers are going to fall out, you can add a little glue.

Once that is done, you are going to wrap the doll baby with the black cloth. Wrap it around the arms and legs as well as the body, until your enemy has been dressed. If you like, you can create a face for your doll baby. That is also an option. Is it needed? Not really. Some folks, however, like to put faces on their doll babies that favor the one they are going to do work on.

When your enemy has been clothed and dressed, it's time to get the holy water. Take the holy water and baptize the doll baby in the name of your enemy. Sprinkle some holy water on his head and say, "I baptize you, John Smith (or whatever the name of your enemy is), in the name of the Father, Son, and Holy Ghost." This further establishes a link between the enemy and the doll baby that will increase the connection for the work to hit. Do you have to be a Christian to do this? No, you do not. The act of baptism is one that is meant to bring a change. The change here is taking a part of the essence of an individual and putting it into another object by way of baptizing it with water, a conduit of the spirit.

Once the sun is fully gone, it's time to go to the graveyard. As we have discussed before, you are going to bring some coins and some rum or whiskey for offerings and make sure your head is covered to protect yourself. You will also need to bring some twine.

When you arrive at the gate, give some coins as an offering to enter the graveyard. After you enter the graveyard, go find a tree inside. It should have some low-hanging branches and be a bit hidden, if possible. When you have found your way over to the tree, you can begin to make offerings there. Throw down some coins and pour out some rum or whiskey at the base of the tree.

Now, you are going to take that doll baby, who is now your enemy, and make your prayers and declarations over it, naming your enemy. You are then going to pray Psalm 35 over that doll baby three times.

35 Plead my cause, O Lord, with them that strive with me: fight against them that fight against me.

2 Take hold of shield and buckler, and stand up for mine help.

3 Draw out also the spear, and stop the way against them that persecute me: say unto my soul, I am thy salvation.

4 Let them be confounded and put to shame that seek after my soul: let them be turned back and brought to confusion that devise my hurt.

5 Let them be as chaff before the wind: and let the angel of the Lord chase them.

6 Let their way be dark and slippery: and let the angel of the Lord persecute them.

7 For without cause have they hid for me their net in a pit, which without cause they have digged for my soul.

8 Let destruction come upon him at unawares; and let his net that he hath hid catch himself: into that very destruction let him fall.

9 And my soul shall be joyful in the Lord: it shall rejoice in his salvation.

10 All my bones shall say, Lord, who is like unto thee, which deliverest the poor from him that is

TOO STRONG FOR HIM, YEA, THE POOR AND THE NEEDY FROM HIM THAT SPOILETH HIM?

11 FALSE WITNESSES DID RISE UP; THEY LAID TO MY CHARGE THINGS THAT I KNEW NOT.

12 THEY REWARDED ME EVIL FOR GOOD TO THE SPOILING OF MY SOUL.

13 BUT AS FOR ME, WHEN THEY WERE SICK, MY CLOTHING WAS SACKCLOTH: I HUMBLED MY SOUL WITH FASTING; AND MY PRAYER RETURNED INTO MINE OWN BOSOM.

14 I BEHAVED MYSELF AS THOUGH HE HAD BEEN MY FRIEND OR BROTHER: I BOWED DOWN HEAVILY, AS ONE THAT MOURNETH FOR HIS MOTHER.

15 BUT IN MINE ADVERSITY THEY REJOICED, AND GATHERED THEMSELVES TOGETHER: YEA, THE ABJECTS GATHERED THEMSELVES TOGETHER AGAINST ME, AND I KNEW IT NOT; THEY DID TEAR ME, AND CEASED NOT:

16 WITH HYPOCRITICAL MOCKERS IN FEASTS, THEY GNASHED UPON ME WITH THEIR TEETH.

17 LORD, HOW LONG WILT THOU LOOK ON? RESCUE MY SOUL FROM THEIR DESTRUCTIONS, MY DARLING FROM THE LIONS.

18 I WILL GIVE THEE THANKS IN THE GREAT CONGREGATION: I WILL PRAISE THEE AMONG MUCH PEOPLE.

19 LET NOT THEM THAT ARE MINE ENEMIES WRONGFULLY REJOICE OVER ME: NEITHER LET THEM WINK WITH THE EYE THAT HATE ME WITHOUT A CAUSE.

20 FOR THEY SPEAK NOT PEACE: BUT THEY DEVISE DECEITFUL MATTERS AGAINST THEM THAT ARE QUIET IN THE LAND.

21 YEA, THEY OPENED THEIR MOUTH WIDE AGAINST ME, AND SAID, AHA, AHA, OUR EYE HATH SEEN IT.

22 THIS THOU HAST SEEN, O LORD: KEEP NOT SILENCE: O LORD, BE NOT FAR FROM ME.

23 STIR UP THYSELF, AND AWAKE TO MY JUDGMENT, EVEN UNTO MY CAUSE, MY GOD AND MY LORD.

24 JUDGE ME, O LORD MY GOD, ACCORDING TO THY RIGHTEOUSNESS; AND LET THEM NOT REJOICE OVER ME.

25 LET THEM NOT SAY IN THEIR HEARTS, AH, SO WOULD WE HAVE IT: LET THEM NOT SAY, WE HAVE SWALLOWED HIM UP.

26 LET THEM BE ASHAMED AND BROUGHT TO CONFUSION TOGETHER THAT REJOICE AT MINE HURT: LET THEM BE CLOTHED WITH SHAME AND DISHONOUR THAT MAGNIFY THEMSELVES AGAINST ME.

27 LET THEM SHOUT FOR JOY, AND BE GLAD, THAT FAVOUR MY RIGHTEOUS CAUSE: YEA, LET THEM SAY CONTINUALLY, LET THE LORD BE MAGNIFIED, WHICH HATH PLEASURE IN THE PROSPERITY OF HIS SERVANT.

28 AND MY TONGUE SHALL SPEAK OF THY RIGHTEOUSNESS AND OF THY PRAISE ALL THE DAY LONG.

After your prayers and declarations have been made, you are going to take that twine and tie up one foot of the doll baby. Then you are going to tie the doll baby to one of the branches of the tree, upside down. When this is done, you are going to make an announcement to the spirits of the graveyard that there is a meal waiting for them. The meal you are referring to is that doll baby. Now, why dangle the doll baby upside down? Well, I'm gonna tell you. As the wind comes and goes, blowing the doll baby back and forth, side to side, and all that, it will make your enemy lose their mind. That, coupled with the work that has been put into it, which is designed to bring defeat and disaster to your enemy, is one trick that ain't no joke.

I will say, should you decide to do this work, don't do it because someone cut you off in traffic or something foolish like that. Our work must always be balanced and justified, so please make sure you work responsibly and not on a whim.

The graveyard holds within it a great power, so please honor and respect it, no matter what work you are doing.

10

WORKINGS FOR
BOTH HANDS

Conjure is and always has been about two things: work and your spirits. The work we do that creates magical change and the relationship with your spirits, your ancestors, and the spirit of the roots is something that must always be at the forefront if you are going to work Conjure and work it effectively. They call it spiritual work for a reason. It is not spiritual easy. I will say, however, that when you are fully embracing the work of Conjure, the culture of Conjure, and the path of Conjure you will most assuredly have a combination of humility and authority that will rival even the fiercest of adversities.

So, what I am going to do is go down a list of works and explain how to do them so you will have some good stuff in your own personal repertoire that will not only bring down the blessings, but also bring up the fire when needed. Ready?

Let's start with some cleansing work. Cleansing is absolutely one of the most important things you can ever do. Not just in Conjure, but in anything. You must go into your work clean and you must clean yourself after. Every time. All the time. If you are not clean when you do your work, there is a good chance that your work will be tainted. The things that are stuck to you will also be stuck on your work. Folks often wonder why things can backfire or lose their potency when they are doing work. Chances are they weren't clean when they started it. You see, if you have things that are stuck to you, then they can influence your work, whether you want them to or not. It would be like using a dirty dish to serve food. Trust and believe that whatever is stuck to that plate is going to fuse with the fresh food put on it.

When you are out and about, going to different places, dealing with different people, their own spiritual influences have the ability to stick to you. Have you ever found that when you are around big crowds of people you may feel drained after? You might have mixed feelings of anger, depression, happiness, and all sorts of other things. This is because other people's spiritual mess can adhere to you. All the more reason to always make sure you do cleansings on the regular.

A WORK FOR SIMPLE CLEANSING (MAINTENANCE)

Ingredients:

- A candle

- A glass of water

- A bottle of Florida Water—great for cleansing

- A couple of pinches of frankincense powder or 10–15 drops frankincense oil—for clearing out evil and allowing for blessings to come into the space

- Enough holy water to fill the empty space in the bottle— for blessings, to remove evil, and to cleanse away spritiual nastiness that can block you

"So, where do I get holy water?" you may ask. I usually get mine from St. Louis Cathedral, one of the Catholic churches here. I just walk into the church and go to the gumbo pot (it looks like a gumbo pot, anyway) where they keep the holy water. I put my offering in the little box they have there and begin to fill up my jar. See, I go and get my holy water in a spaghetti sauce jar. I always seem to get funny looks when folks in the church see me filling up my empty Prego jar. That's the thing, it doesn't matter what it is contained in, just that you have it. Conjure folk are very practical people, we use what's around.

If you do not want to go into a church to get the holy water or you do not have access to a church, there are many spiritual supply stores, botanicas, and the like that carry it.

As with all this work, start with a lit candle and a glass of water nearby, and present each item to the four directions before you begin.

Take the bottle of Florida Water and pour a little bit of it out so you have space for the other ingredients. You can pour it into a heat-resistant container and burn it as an offering to your ancestors if you like. That is what I do.

Next, you are going to put the frankincense into the bottle.

After you have done that, fill the rest of the bottle with holy water. Usually, the Florida Water will turn a milky white color when you do that. After that, shake it up and then you can make your prayers over it.

These prayers will be for keeping evil off of and away from you, to be cleansed every time you use it, for protection, and for peace to follow your footsteps. Some of the best Psalms for this are Psalm 51 (page 41) and Psalm 108. You should begin with Psalm 51, praying it three times over the bottle. Once that is finished, pray Psalm 108 three times over the bottle. Psalm 108 is great for protection and victory over enemies. The potency of protection and victory is what you should be walking in on a daily basis. Psalm 108:

108 O GOD, MY HEART IS FIXED; I WILL SING AND GIVE PRAISE, EVEN WITH MY GLORY.

2 AWAKE, PSALTERY AND HARP: I MYSELF WILL AWAKE EARLY.

3 I WILL PRAISE THEE, O LORD, AMONG THE PEOPLE: AND I WILL SING PRAISES UNTO THEE AMONG THE NATIONS.

4 FOR THY MERCY IS GREAT ABOVE THE HEAVENS: AND THY TRUTH REACHETH UNTO THE CLOUDS.

5 BE THOU EXALTED, O GOD, ABOVE THE HEAVENS: AND THY GLORY ABOVE ALL THE EARTH;

6 THAT THY BELOVED MAY BE DELIVERED: SAVE WITH THY RIGHT HAND, AND ANSWER ME.

7 GOD HATH SPOKEN IN HIS HOLINESS; I WILL REJOICE, I WILL DIVIDE SHECHEM, AND METE OUT THE VALLEY OF SUCCOTH.

8 GILEAD IS MINE; MANASSEH IS MINE; EPHRAIM ALSO IS THE STRENGTH OF MINE HEAD; JUDAH IS MY LAWGIVER;

9 MOAB IS MY WASHPOT; OVER EDOM WILL I CAST OUT MY SHOE; OVER PHILISTIA WILL I TRIUMPH.

10 WHO WILL BRING ME INTO THE STRONG CITY? WHO WILL LEAD ME INTO EDOM?

11 WILT NOT THOU, O GOD, WHO HAST CAST US OFF? AND WILT NOT THOU, O GOD, GO FORTH WITH OUR HOSTS?

12 GIVE US HELP FROM TROUBLE: FOR VAIN IS THE HELP OF MAN.

13 THROUGH GOD WE SHALL DO VALIANTLY: FOR HE IT
IS THAT SHALL TREAD DOWN OUR ENEMIES.

Once you have prayed those prayers three times apiece, then make some petitions to your ancestors—that they will help to cleanse and walk with you, that they will protect you, and that they will give you blessings in your day.

Now that the bottle is done you can begin to apply it. As was mentioned in chapter 9 (page 89), you will want to put in on your forehead, the back of your neck, your heart, your hands, and your feet.

You put it on your head because your head carries your spirit in it. Your head also can be a holding area of spiritual mud so it must be cleansed and protected always.

The back of your neck is a sensitive area for the spirit. That can be both good and bad. The back of the neck is also a place where burdens rest as if you are carrying a yoke. It is one of the most important places on your body that needs to be cleansed on the regular.

Your heart is the place that runs your body. It also carries burdens of the emotions, stress of the mind and spirit, as well as being the central point of who you are. The heart holds a special place, not only in your work, but also in your growth.

Your hands are what you work with. They are used both to create and to destroy. The hands also are a place where your spirits work through you to carry out deeds of the physical and deeds of the spiritual. It is with the hands that we do the work that creates magical change.

Your feet are what carry you in your walk. They bring you from point to point and are your primary mode of transportation, both literally and figuratively. You walk in the spirit and walk in the physical. It is by your feet that you walk the path.

These points are all very important to keep clean. The cleaner they are, the easier it is to do all of the things you need to do and to receive the blessings that are meant for you.

If you make it a point to use this cleansing on yourself daily, things will seem much easier in general and you won't feel like you are walking through the mud as much. That opens the door for you to focus on the things that are going to push you forward and help you grow.

A FLOOR WASH TO CLEANSE YOUR HOUSE

Your home is your sanctuary and should be one of the most potent places that holds your work. If your home is not drawing in the things you are trying to work, the blessings you are trying to receive, or the spirit of your own prosperity, you might want to change that. If the space you live in is not a reflection of your own work then how would you expect to hold all of the spiritual blessings that are trying to come to you?

What I am trying to say here is that if your house isn't clean then it will have the strong potential to affect your work, in particular, the work you are doing for yourself. So, we are going to go over a floor wash that you can use not only to clean your house both physically and spiritually, but also to draw in blessings.

As I have said before, Conjure is extremely hands-on and practical. We are always looking at the crossroads and reflecting the mirror of the physical into the mirror of the spiritual and vice versa. In other words, just because you see me washing the floor doesn't mean that is the only thing I am doing. Trust and believe that if I am washing the floor, the physical cleaning of it is only one part of what is actually happening. I am working blessings, drawing in my spirits, and removing the spiritual muck and mud that have tracked through my house.

Ingredients:

- A lit candle

- A glass of water

- 2 cups of pine bark or a handful of green needles (*Pinus*); (you can use pine oil [1–1½ ounces] if you can't get actual pine)—for potent physical and spiritual cleansing

- ½ cup Solomon's seal root (*Polygonatum biflorum*)—for commanding and a spirit of direction to focus other roots

- ½ cup angelica root—for protection and cleansing

- 1–1½ cups lime juice (*Citrus aurantifolia*)—for cleansing, breaking work that has been done, and removing negativity

- A medium-size pot

- ¾ of a pot full of water from a river while it is moving away from you—for moving away foolishness and things that have built up to taint your house

- 4–5 tablespoons Epsom salt—for cleansing

- A couple of cups of high-proof rum—for use as a preservative and an offering

- Florida Water (optional)

- A new mop

So, what you are going to do is get a candle set and a glass of water, take the roots, present them to the four directions, then begin to make your petitions and prayers over them. Your petitions and prayers should be prayers of cleansing as well as protection in your house. You should petition the roots to remove the spiritual buildup of mud and negativity, apathy, and whatever else may be lingering around. A great prayer to use for this is Psalm 29. It is a Psalm that is prayed for victory and peace. The victory here would be your home being cleansed and filled with peace.

29 GIVE UNTO THE LORD, O YE MIGHTY, GIVE UNTO THE LORD GLORY AND STRENGTH.

2 GIVE UNTO THE LORD THE GLORY DUE UNTO HIS NAME; WORSHIP THE LORD IN THE BEAUTY OF HOLINESS.

3 THE VOICE OF THE LORD IS UPON THE WATERS: THE GOD OF GLORY THUNDERETH: THE LORD IS UPON MANY WATERS.

4 THE VOICE OF THE LORD IS POWERFUL; THE VOICE OF THE LORD IS FULL OF MAJESTY.

5 THE VOICE OF THE LORD BREAKETH THE CEDARS; YEA, THE LORD BREAKETH THE CEDARS OF LEBANON.

6 HE MAKETH THEM ALSO TO SKIP LIKE A CALF; LEBANON AND SIRION LIKE A YOUNG UNICORN.

7 THE VOICE OF THE LORD DIVIDETH THE FLAMES OF FIRE.

8 THE VOICE OF THE LORD SHAKETH THE WILDERNESS; THE LORD SHAKETH THE WILDERNESS OF KADESH.

9 THE VOICE OF THE LORD MAKETH THE HINDS TO CALVE, AND DISCOVERETH THE FORESTS: AND IN HIS TEMPLE DOTH EVERY ONE SPEAK OF HIS GLORY.

10 THE LORD SITTETH UPON THE FLOOD; YEA, THE LORD SITTETH KING FOR EVER.

11 THE LORD WILL GIVE STRENGTH UNTO HIS PEOPLE; THE LORD WILL BLESS HIS PEOPLE WITH PEACE.

This prayer is great to pray when you are doing this work because sometimes, even within our own homes, we have to battle with the foolishness that has allowed itself to slip in, and kill it. Pray the Psalm over the roots three times and, of course, make your own petitions as well. The three times is to complete a cycle. Some folks pray three times for the Holy Trinity. Regardless, you are praying in the beginning, in the middle, and in the end.

Once your prayers and offerings have been made, you can go ahead and get out the pot, put it on the stove, and fill it about three-quarters to the top with the water from the river, then turn on the stove.

Next, put the Epsom salt into the water. Aside from being very good in cleansing work, Epsom salt is also a preservative. Doing this work, I would not want to make just one wash, but I would rather make a batch that I could use later when it was time to clean again. Makes sense, yeah?

Add that rum into the water.

Once the water is heating up, add your roots and continue to make your prayers. You should be making prayers and petitions while you are stirring the pot. In this case, you are stirring a pot that is going to cleanse your house both physically and spiritually, so get those prayers working.

It should boil for about ten minutes or so before you take it off the heat.

Once it is done, you can add some Florida Water to the mix if you like (that is completely up to you).

You are then going to take the roots out of the pot and put them on a separate plate. There will be some remnants of the roots in the batch and that is ok. Leave a little there.

When you have finished straining the roots out, you can take the wash and put it in a jug or jar or other container.

To make your mop water, take some hot water and put it in a bucket. Add about three cups of the floor wash per gallon of water. You will need to use a new mop for this because you don't want anything that may be on the old mop to taint the work.

Once your water is finished and you have your mop ready, you can begin to cleanse your house. You want to start at the back of the house and move to the front. The reason for this is because you are going to be pushing out all of the negativity and spiritual muck through the same door it came in. While you are mopping you are continuing to make your petitions and prayers. You are going to declare your home is being cleansed and that no spiritual muck is going to remain. The petitions and the mopping together bring the cleansing, you see. It is not only in your deed, but also in your work. If you have a house with more than one floor, begin at the top floor and work your way down.

When you have finished mopping and cleansing your house, take the mop water and throw it out your front door. If you have steps, throw it on the steps. That mop water is made for cleansing and is just as good outside as it is good inside.

Now, those roots you put on that plate when you were straining them from the mop water, you want to go get them. Take them to the front door and sprinkle them outside. If you have a door mat you can put some of them under the mat. The rest of the roots can be put on your steps, porch, or whatever you have outside your front door. The roots will continue to work even after you are finished. Sprinkling them out the front door will help with keeping that spiritual muck outside. It is an additional measure that you take to keep your sanctuary cleansed and peaceful.

A WORK FOR PROSPERITY (A CONJURE PACKET)

One of my favorite roots is that of thyme. Thyme is a drawing root that is used to attract prosperity—particularly money. This work is something that you will keep in your wallet to keep money coming into it.

Ingredients:

- A candle
- A glass of water
- A one-dollar bill
- A few pinches of thyme
- Glue or wax to seal the packet
- Some green or gold thread
- A piece of an orange peel

As I have explained before, you must always give offerings to the roots. See chapter 4 for a refresher, if you need to.

Once the offerings and such have been made for everything, you can begin your prayers and petitions. In this case, you are going to be making petitions of prosperity, declarations of never having an empty wallet and having a constant drawing of money coming to you. When I make these workings, I also pray Psalm 118 three times. This Psalm is great for prosperity, for victory, and for walking in divine favor.

118 O GIVE THANKS UNTO THE LORD; FOR HE IS GOOD: BECAUSE HIS MERCY ENDURETH FOR EVER.

2 LET ISRAEL NOW SAY, THAT HIS MERCY ENDURETH FOR EVER.

3 LET THE HOUSE OF AARON NOW SAY, THAT HIS MERCY ENDURETH FOR EVER.

4 LET THEM NOW THAT FEAR THE LORD SAY, THAT HIS MERCY ENDURETH FOR EVER.

5 I CALLED UPON THE LORD IN DISTRESS: THE LORD ANSWERED ME, AND SET ME IN A LARGE PLACE.

6 THE LORD IS ON MY SIDE; I WILL NOT FEAR: WHAT CAN MAN DO UNTO ME?

7 THE LORD TAKETH MY PART WITH THEM THAT HELP ME: THEREFORE SHALL I SEE MY DESIRE UPON THEM THAT HATE ME.

8 IT IS BETTER TO TRUST IN THE LORD THAN TO PUT CONFIDENCE IN MAN.

9 IT IS BETTER TO TRUST IN THE LORD THAN TO PUT CONFIDENCE IN PRINCES.

10 ALL NATIONS COMPASSED ME ABOUT: BUT IN THE NAME OF THE LORD WILL I DESTROY THEM.

11 THEY COMPASSED ME ABOUT; YEA, THEY COMPASSED ME ABOUT: BUT IN THE NAME OF THE LORD I WILL DESTROY THEM.

12 THEY COMPASSED ME ABOUT LIKE BEES: THEY ARE QUENCHED AS THE FIRE OF THORNS: FOR IN THE NAME OF THE LORD I WILL DESTROY THEM.

13 THOU HAST THRUST SORE AT ME THAT I MIGHT FALL: BUT THE LORD HELPED ME.

14 THE LORD IS MY STRENGTH AND SONG, AND IS BECOME MY SALVATION.

15 THE VOICE OF REJOICING AND SALVATION IS IN THE TABERNACLES OF THE RIGHTEOUS: THE RIGHT HAND OF THE LORD DOETH VALIANTLY.

16 THE RIGHT HAND OF THE LORD IS EXALTED: THE RIGHT HAND OF THE LORD DOETH VALIANTLY.

17 I SHALL NOT DIE, BUT LIVE, AND DECLARE THE WORKS OF THE LORD.

18 THE LORD HATH CHASTENED ME SORE: BUT HE HATH NOT GIVEN ME OVER UNTO DEATH.

19 OPEN TO ME THE GATES OF RIGHTEOUSNESS: I WILL GO INTO THEM, AND I WILL PRAISE THE LORD:

20 THIS GATE OF THE LORD, INTO WHICH THE RIGHTEOUS SHALL ENTER.

21 I WILL PRAISE THEE: FOR THOU HAST HEARD ME, AND ART BECOME MY SALVATION.

22 THE STONE WHICH THE BUILDERS REFUSED IS BECOME THE HEAD STONE OF THE CORNER.

23 THIS IS THE LORD'S DOING; IT IS MARVELLOUS IN OUR EYES.

24 THIS IS THE DAY WHICH THE LORD HATH MADE; WE WILL REJOICE AND BE GLAD IN IT.

25 SAVE NOW, I BESEECH THEE, O LORD: O LORD, I BESEECH THEE, SEND NOW PROSPERITY.

26 BLESSED BE HE THAT COMETH IN THE NAME OF THE LORD: WE HAVE BLESSED YOU OUT OF THE HOUSE OF THE LORD.

27 GOD IS THE LORD, WHICH HATH SHEWED US LIGHT: BIND THE SACRIFICE WITH CORDS, EVEN UNTO THE HORNS OF THE ALTAR.

28 THOU ART MY GOD, AND I WILL PRAISE THEE: THOU ART MY GOD, I WILL EXALT THEE.

29 O GIVE THANKS UNTO THE LORD; FOR HE IS GOOD:
FOR HIS MERCY ENDURETH FOR EVER.

When the prayers and petitions are done, you are going to take the one-dollar bill and put it with the pyramid and eye facing down toward the work surface.

Put the thyme on top of the dollar bill, right above where the pyramid and eye are located on the other side of the bill.

Next, you are going to fold the sides of the dollar bill over the thyme, making a small packet. You can use glue or wax to seal it, whichever you prefer.

When the packet is made, you are going to bind it up on all four sides with the string. When you are binding it, you are going to wrap the string toward you, because you are drawing to yourself. Wrap each side so that it forms a square around the pyramid and eye. After you bind each side, tie seven knots in the string. The seven knots are the completion of a cycle and, in this case, the completion of the work.

Now that your packet is made, you are going to give it offerings—feeding it, giving it smoke and either rum or whiskey. Blow the smoke and pour the rum or whiskey onto it.

Next you are going to make your declarations over the work—that it will be a constant draw of prosperity and money.

When it is done, put it in your wallet with the eye of the pyramid facing out when the wallet is closed. See, the eye draws toward you and works with the roots to bring money into your wallet.

A WORK TO OPEN UP THE ROADS

Road-opening work is something that holds a high place of importance in Conjure. It is the crossroads that opens up our opportunities, blessings, luck, prosperity, and literally our paths.

It is also the crossroads that can shut them all down. The crossroads truly is one of the most powerful places in this world.

Ingredients:

- A written petition
- A trowel
- Some coins for the spirits, plus a few more for the ground (a quarter, a dime, a nickel, and a penny should be just fine for each)
- A cigar
- A match or lighter
- At least a shot glass worth of rum or whiskey, plus a little more
- Some candy

First, you need to write out on a petition a prayer that your roads will be open, that your opportunities will rise up, that your blessings will come freely and without adversity, and that your path will be clear. You can make the prayer any way you like. Remember, you are going to be doing work to open up the roads for yourself, so keep that in mind when writing your petition.

After the petition is written, you are going to take all of the ingredients to the crossroads. Any crossroads will do, as long as there is dirt somewhere around where you can dig a small hole. A good time to do this work is during the transition time, when the sun is rising. The transition of the spirit to the living is the transition of the dawn and this work is actually beginning in the spirit and moving into the flesh.

When you get to the crossroads, the first thing you are going to do is toss some coins into the middle of it as an offering for the spirits.

Once that is done, you can dig a small hole.

When the hole is dug, you are going to put the remaining coins in it. You have to pay the earth as well, you know.

After you have paid the crossroads and the ground, you are going to get your petition out. This is when you begin to pray out loud the petition you wrote. You need to pray it with all of your inner strength, knowing that you are about to open up the roads in your life. Pray the petition three times.

Once you have done that, hold the petition in your hand. Get out the cigar to make an offering for the work by giving your petition some smoke.

After you have given the offering of smoke, you can go ahead and set the petition in the hole you dug. You should continue making your declarations over your work while doing this— steadily making those prayers of open roads, of blessings, and of a clear path for yourself.

Now, you are going to take the rum or whiskey and pour it into the hole, on top of your petition.

When the libation has been poured out, you are going to put in the candy. Candy is an offering that can be used to sweeten up a situation.

Once the candy is put into the hole, you can go ahead and bury the petition, filling the hole back up with the dirt you took out of it.

After the hole is filled, you are going to take some more rum or whiskey and pour it over it. When that is done, you are going to give thanks for the work and for what is about to go down, and walk away. Personally, I love this work because it definitely brings about change.

A WORK OF FAST LUCK

This work is good to draw luck to you and the things that you are doing. Fast luck work is like using a magnet to bring luck and opportunities to you. Who can't use a little luck in their work?

Ingredients:

- 1 candle to light the way, plus 14 small one-hour emergency candles
- 1 glass of water—to act as a conduit for the spirits
- 5 small plates or bowls (one for each ingredient)
- 3 cinnamon sticks—to heat up the work
- 3 tablespoons bayberry root (*Myrica pensylvanica*)—to bring money to you
- 3 tablespoons arrowroot powder (*Maranta arundinacea*)—to open doors of luck
- 1 High John the Conqueror root—for tearing down that which stands in your way
- A bit of bayberry oil—for scent (optional)
- 1 magnet—to draw things toward you
- A few drops of rum or whiskey for each ingredient, plus 2–3 caps full
- 1 cigar or cigarette—for smoke
- 1 pint-size Mason jar
- Approximately 1 pint of olive oil—to add a spirit of peace and to bring spirits to the work

To fix a candle with the oil you will also need:

- A small photo of yourself or a bit of your own hair or nail clippings

Now, I am about to tell you how to make Fast Luck Oil. This oil, when made right, can change anything for the better. The boost of luck to change circumstances and situations is one that so many folks are looking for, so why not give it to you? If I can do one thing here, it is to empower you to be able to work magical change in your life. That is one of the cornerstone reasons for Conjure, after all.

Once the light is set and the glass of water is at your work space, you are going to get all your ingredients together. You need to have each one on a separate little plate or dish, as it's not time to bring them together. Once you have them all on their dishes or bowls, it's time to begin to make your offerings.

First, present each of the ingredients to the four directions.

Next, take some rum or whiskey and give it to the roots. You can blow it on the roots if you like or you can pour a few drops on them. For the High John root, however, you will need to soak it in a couple of caps full of the rum or whiskey. It softens the root, which is typically very dense and hard.

Once that is done you are going to give offerings of smoke to the roots.

When you have finished making your offerings to the roots, it is time for you to make your prayers and petitions over them—prayers of luck coming to your side, petitions of luck being drawn to you like a magnet. Psalm 4 is not only great for increase, for opportunity, but also has built-in protection for your work.

4 Hear me when I call, O God of my righteousness: thou hast enlarged me when I was in distress; have mercy upon me, and hear my prayer.

2 O ye sons of men, how long will ye turn my glory into shame? how long will ye love vanity, and seek after leasing? Selah.

3 But know that the Lord hath set apart him that is godly for himself: the Lord will hear when I call unto him.

4 Stand in awe, and sin not: commune with your own heart upon your bed, and be still. Selah.

5 Offer the sacrifices of righteousness, and put your trust in the Lord.

6 There be many that say, Who will shew us any good? Lord, lift thou up the light of thy countenance upon us.

7 Thou hast put gladness in my heart, more than in the time that their corn and their wine increased.

8 I will both lay me down in peace, and sleep: for thou, Lord, only makest me dwell in safety.

You should pray this Psalm three times over your work. Again, the Psalms are a powerful petition and prayer that not only increase the potency of your work, but also open up the door for that magic to manifest.

After your petitions and prayers have been completed, you are going to leave the roots there at the work space or altar for a day. Make sure you keep a light on your work because it will continue to work even after you are finished for the day.

So, the next day, you will return to the work and make your petitions and prayers again. However, this time you are going to speak to each root individually as well. Basically, you are giving them their job to do.

After you have finished making your petitions for that day, keep the light on the work for the following day. Now, on day three, you are going to continue your petitions and prayers. Once they are finished you are going to bring the roots together. Take a mortar and pestle and begin to crush them into each other. The only root you will not crush will be the High John root. This root needs to remain whole because you want the full wrecking ball in your corner. While you are crushing them together, you will continue to make your declarations of the work, that luck is being drawn to you and that you are a magnet of fast luck.

When this part is finished, you are going to pour the ingredients into the jar. The roots will go in first. Then you will pour enough olive oil on top of them to fill the jar. If you like, you can add some bayberry oil for scent. You will find that it mixes nicely with the cinnamon.

When the jar is full and all the roots are in it, go ahead and close the lid. Then you are going to shake the jar, continuing to make your prayers and petitions over it. Each day, for fourteen days, you are going to shake the jar and burn a candle on top of it.

Once the fourteen-day period is over, you will have a batch of Fast Luck oil that, if I say so myself, is quite potent. If you would like to make it extra potent you can take it to a crossroads or a casino and bury it there for three days after it is finished. Remember, the dirts hold power and you can absolutely use it to increase the potency of your own work.

When your oil is ready, you can use it to fix a candle or you can dress yourself with it. If you dress yourself with it, you are going to take a few drops of the oil and put it into the palm of your left hand if you are right-handed or your right hand if you are left-handed.

Whichever hand you put the drops in will then be covered by the other hand. Then you are going to rub the oil from your palm toward your forearm and make petitions or prayers of luck being drawn and attracted to you. You can say something simple. For example, while you are rubbing the oil toward your forearm you can say, "Luck is drawing itself to me; I am a magnet for luck; let me be blessed with luck and opportunity today."

So, with that, you can use the oil to draw that luck into yourself and see what goes down! Trust and believe, this oil is one that many folks have had great success with and is one of the things I swear by.

The same principle is used if you are fixing a candle with it.

The only other thing you would need to do is add yourself to the candle. An easy and very effective way to do that is to take a little photo of yourself and burn it into ash. Rub the ash into the candle to establish that personal link. If you like, you can also fix the candle with your own hair or nail clippings. The only thing that matters here is that the candle you are going to fix for fast luck has a link to you. Do the work and let the work be done!

FIXED RAILROAD SPIKES TO FORTIFY YOUR HOUSE

Your home, as I have said before, is your sanctuary. It is the place where you should always find peace, shelter, and comfort. The home should also be a place that is heavily protected. Oftentimes, you may be so busy in other things that wards and such will slip your mind. This is something that allows for foolishness to creep in and the devil to run wild in your house, so to speak. Here is a work that will help to fortify your home and keep good and hot protections in place.

Ingredients:

- A candle

- A glass of water

- 4 railroad spikes—for a strong and assertive spirit that acts like a bodyguard

- A heat-resistant bowl, pan, pot, or cauldron big enough to hold the spikes

- Some Florida Water—for cleansing as well as protection and for use as an offering

- Some red twine—for protection assistance from Michael the Archangel who has an affinity for the color red

- A bit of rum or whiskey for each spike

If you live in an apartment, you will also need:

- 4 flowerpots big enough to hold the spikes

- Dirt to fill the pots (at least a handful must be from the property)

- Plants to put in the pots (optional)

When you have everything together, you are going to take the spikes and put them in the pan.

Next, pour some Florida Water on them.

When that is done you are going to light the spikes on fire. Make sure you do it in a place where you can have a little fire; y'all don't need to be having any accidents!

When the spikes are lit and burning, you are going to begin your prayers and petitions over them. Two prayers you should pray three times over the spikes are the 91st Psalm and the prayer of Michael the Archangel. If you haven't noticed, Psalm 91 is one of my favorites and packs a punch for protection as well. Here are the prayers, starting with Psalm 91:

91 HE THAT DWELLETH IN THE SECRET PLACE OF THE MOST HIGH SHALL ABIDE UNDER THE SHADOW OF THE ALMIGHTY.

2 I WILL SAY OF THE LORD, HE IS MY REFUGE AND MY FORTRESS: MY GOD; IN HIM WILL I TRUST.

3 Surely he shall deliver thee from the snare of the fowler, and from the noisome pestilence.

4 He shall cover thee with his feathers, and under his wings shalt thou trust: his truth shall be thy shield and buckler.

5 Thou shalt not be afraid for the terror by night; nor for the arrow that flieth by day;

6 Nor for the pestilence that walketh in darkness; nor for the destruction that wasteth at noonday.

7 A thousand shall fall at thy side, and ten thousand at thy right hand; but it shall not come nigh thee.

8 Only with thine eyes shalt thou behold and see the reward of the wicked.

9 Because thou hast made the Lord, which is my refuge, even the most High, thy habitation;

10 There shall no evil befall thee, neither shall any plague come nigh thy dwelling.

11 For he shall give his angels charge over thee, to keep thee in all thy ways.

12 They shall bear thee up in their hands, lest thou dash thy foot against a stone.

13 Thou shalt tread upon the lion and adder: the young lion and the dragon shalt thou trample under feet.

14 Because he hath set his love upon me, therefore will I deliver him: I will set him on high, because he hath known my name.

15 HE SHALL CALL UPON ME, AND I WILL ANSWER HIM:
I WILL BE WITH HIM IN TROUBLE; I WILL DELIVER
HIM, AND HONOUR HIM.

16 WITH LONG LIFE WILL I SATISFY HIM, AND SHEW
HIM MY SALVATION.

And here is a prayer for Michael the Archangel:

MICHAEL, ARCHANGEL OF GOD, I COME TO YOU AND
ASK FOR YOUR AID. YOU, WHO ARE A GREAT DEFENDER
AND TRIUMPHANT WARRIOR IN BATTLE, AID ME IN THIS
PROTECTION WORK, I HUMBLY PRAY. I COME TO YOU AND
ASK THAT YOUR DIVINE HAND TOUCH AND HEAT THIS
WORK SO THAT NO EVIL WILL BEFALL ME OR MY HOME. I
ASK THAT YOU STAND BEFORE ME, BEING A SHIELD AND
DEFENDER IN ALL I DO. THE POWER OF GOD THAT YOU
HOLD, PLEASE, MICHAEL, USE IT IN MY DEFENSE. I THANK
YOU FOR HEARING ME, FOR AIDING ME, AND FOR STAND-
ING IN THE PLACE OF PROTECTION FOR ME. AMEN.

When you have finished these prayers, you are going to pray
and petition for protection, specifically for your home, you,
and those who live there, as well as any person or persons who
come there—that your home will be fortified and that no evil
or malevolent work is able to come onto your place.

See, the thing is that while you are making these prayers
and petitions, you are doing work that is made to stop negative influences and spirits from coming into your sanctuary,
your home. Know that as you are making these prayers, you
are making a magical change that will affect not only the spirit
of your house in general, but also the spirit of those who come
there. Don't just go through the motions and expect change to
happen. Feel the prayers and petitions in your heart. You decide
what you allow into your fortress, your sanctuary, so make sure

that everyone and everything else knows that too. How do you do that? When you speak from your heart and merge yourself with your work, you create a power that pushes the work forward and when someone comes around your home they're gonna feel it! Trust and believe that.

So, when the prayers have been made and the fire has gone out on the spikes and they are cool enough to touch, you are going to bind them with the red twine. Begin by tying a knot around the top of the spike with the twine, so it stays in place. Then, wrap the twine toward you around the spike. The reason for this is because you are calling protection to yourself and your home. While you are wrapping the spikes, you are going to continue to make those petitions of protection. Wrap the spikes all the way down to the point.

When you reach the point, you are going to continue to wrap all the way back up to the top of each spike. When you have finished that you are going to tie the twine in seven knots at the top. The seven knots are the completion of a cycle and set the stage for a new beginning of protection in your home and those who dwell there.

Once that is done, give the spikes an offering of a little rum or whiskey. Just pour a bit on each spike and that will be just fine.

After that is done, you are going to take the spikes and plant them outside, one at each of the four corners of your house or property. Take the spikes and push them into the ground. When you do this you are nailing down protection in your house and property.

If you live in an apartment where you feel you can't plant the spikes outside, fill the four flowerpots with dirt. Plant one spike in each pot and put one pot in each corner of your home and those protections will work that way. You can also plant some flowers or other plants in the pots if you like. The point is that the spikes are planted so that protection is nailed down in your home.

Once you have done that, give thanks to your ancestors, to your spirits, and allow the work to begin to fortify your home. You will need to give those spikes some offerings about once every two or three months. As they continue to work they should continue to receive offerings. Simply pour some rum or whiskey on them and make a prayer or petition over them for continued protection. As you continue to work and honor the work that is being done, the work will also honor you by continuing to be steadfast in the job that it is doing.

A PROTECTION BATH

Baths are something we use in Conjure quite a bit. The bath can draw things to you as well as take things off of you. The nature of a bath is one that, no matter the work, has a cleansing element to it—whether for the body or the body and the spirit. This bath will draw protection to you in your day-to-day activities.

Why would you need a protection bath? Well, remember that anytime you are out and about, whether it's at work, in a social setting, or simply running errands, you are around other folks who may have things on them that can have an effect on you. Also, you never know what can happen while you are out in the world. As a rule, protection should always be in place for you. It should always be consistent and you should always be working in that regard.

ooooo

Ingredients:

- A glass of water

- 1 candle, plus 1 white candle—to light the path

138

- A plate

- 1 High John the Conqueror root—to protect by busting up foolishness that crosses your path

- 2 large pinches of angelica root—to cleanse and protect by stopping negative things before they reach you

- 3 bay leaves (*Laurus nobilis*)—to shield you from being hit with negativity and work that someone may be throwing at you

- 2 large pinches of Low John root (*Trillium pendulum*)

- Some rum or whiskey, plus an additional ½ cup

- A cigar or cigarette for smoke

- A medium-size pot

- Water

- Some Florida Water—to repel murky, muddy spirits that may try to suck on you like a leech

Once you have everything together—make sure you have a candle burning and a glass of water present—take the roots and put them on a plate. Keep them separated on the plate at first.

Next, you are going to give them offerings and orient the roots to the four directions.

When the offerings have been given, you are going to begin to make your prayers and petitions over the roots. You are going to speak protection over yourself and petition the roots to perform the job of protecting you, of making a wall of protection around you.

The declarations made and the prayers prayed are like giving direction to the roots about what their job is and what they are being asked to do. You can pray over them from your heart as well as use other prayers. The more you put into the work, the more potent it becomes.

After you have made your prayers and petitions, get the pot. You are going to put some water into it and put it on the stove.

When you put the pot on the stove, put some Florida Water in it.

You are also going to add the extra rum or whiskey to the water in the pot.

Let the water heat up, then add your roots to it. As you are adding the roots to it, speak to them individually and tell them their job. For example, speak to the angelica root and tell it that it has the job of going before you to be the guardian that stops negative muck from sticking to you. Speak to the bay and tell it that its job is to be a shield that stands between you and anything that may try to hinder the work at hand. Just as we work with the spirits of our ancestors, we also work with the spirits of the roots. They are old, potent, and very much a part of this work. It is very important to always acknowledge that, because it is their help we are seeking, after all.

While the water is heating up with the roots in it, you are going to stir all the roots together inside the pot. As you are stirring it together, continue to make those petitions over the pot. You continue to work in creating the bath that will become a shield and a force of protection with a barrier that not a damn thing will be able to penetrate. When you stand strong in your work, your work stands strong in you.

After about ten minutes or so, after the water has changed color, you are going to take the roots and the water to the bathtub. You can scoop some of the roots out beforehand if you like, but some of them need to be present in the tub. Draw a very warm bath and make sure to have the white candle lit and present in the bathroom.

You are going to take the pot and pour it into the bathtub. When that's done, go ahead and get in.

Now, when you get into the tub, you are going to begin to wash yourself from the feet upward. Why? The reason for this is that the protection bath is made for you to draw protection to yourself. By washing from the feet up, you are drawing into yourself the protection you are looking for.

While you are in the tub, you need to continue to make your petitions and declarations of protection over yourself. As you wash, you are going to feel the spirits of the roots doing their work and you need to continue to make those declarations so that the work is as strong as it needs to be. You should be in the tub about ten to fifteen minutes taking the bath. When you are finished, you are going to let the water out and you should drip-dry so the bath can soak into the skin.

Once the bath is done and you are out of the tub, give thanks to your spirits and the spirits of the roots, and let the protection you just set on yourself do its job.

A WATCHER AND PROTECTOR AGAINST THE EVIL EYE

The evil eye is something that has a whole lot of influence that can trip folks up, whether they actively realize it or not. A lot of the time it is birthed out of some sort of envy, jealousy, or offense taken that makes a person look at you with a heart of destruction. If you have something someone wants and they don't want to go and get it themselves, they may impose their own jealousy on you or manifest their own backbiting envy into your presence. Well, let me tell ya, envy, jealousy, and being offended are the fuel, and the eye is the direction in which it is thrown. I will always say that you can never have too much protection around and this is one way to stop the work of the evil eye from coming in your home.

Ingredients:

- A white candle—to light the way

- A small glass of water—to drown the eye

- A few drops of holy water (optional)

- 3 evil eye beads—to catch the evil eye when it is thrown

- A cube of camphor (*Cinnamomum camphora*)—to cleanse the area and keep it clean

Have a candle going to light the way.

Take a small glass and fill it with water. Adding a few drops of holy water certainly won't hurt it.

When you have that all together, you are going to take the glass of water and present it to the four directions because you are sending the work out to every corner of the world.

Once that is done you are going to take the evil eye beads and put them inside of the glass. The evil eye cannot survive under the water.

Once the eyes are in the water then you are going to get that cube of camphor and put it in the glass. The camphor is going to float at the top of the glass and continue to do its job of cleansing.

Now, you are going to begin to make your prayers and petitions over the work. For this work, Psalm 37 is a potent prayer for protection and to stop work being done against you. You are going to pray this Psalm three times over the work and then make your specific petitions. Psalm 37:

37 Fret not thyself because of evildoers, neither be thou envious against the workers of iniquity.

2 For they shall soon be cut down like the grass, and wither as the green herb.

3 Trust in the Lord, and do good; so shalt thou dwell in the land, and verily thou shalt be fed.

4 Delight thyself also in the Lord: and he shall give thee the desires of thine heart.

5 Commit thy way unto the Lord; trust also in him; and he shall bring it to pass.

6 And he shall bring forth thy righteousness as the light, and thy judgment as the noonday.

7 Rest in the Lord, and wait patiently for him: fret not thyself because of him who prospereth in his way, because of the man who bringeth wicked devices to pass.

8 Cease from anger, and forsake wrath: fret not thyself in any wise to do evil.

9 For evildoers shall be cut off: but those that wait upon the Lord, they shall inherit the earth.

10 For yet a little while, and the wicked shall not be: yea, thou shalt diligently consider his place, and it shall not be.

11 But the meek shall inherit the earth; and shall delight themselves in the abundance of peace.

12 The wicked plotteth against the just, and gnasheth upon him with his teeth.

13 The Lord shall laugh at him: for he seeth that his day is coming.

14 THE WICKED HAVE DRAWN OUT THE SWORD, AND
HAVE BENT THEIR BOW, TO CAST DOWN THE POOR
AND NEEDY, AND TO SLAY SUCH AS BE OF UPRIGHT
CONVERSATION.

15 THEIR SWORD SHALL ENTER INTO THEIR OWN HEART,
AND THEIR BOWS SHALL BE BROKEN.

16 A LITTLE THAT A RIGHTEOUS MAN HATH IS BETTER
THAN THE RICHES OF MANY WICKED.

17 FOR THE ARMS OF THE WICKED SHALL BE BROKEN:
BUT THE LORD UPHOLDETH THE RIGHTEOUS.

18 THE LORD KNOWETH THE DAYS OF THE UPRIGHT:
AND THEIR INHERITANCE SHALL BE FOR EVER.

19 THEY SHALL NOT BE ASHAMED IN THE EVIL TIME:
AND IN THE DAYS OF FAMINE THEY SHALL BE SATISFIED.

20 BUT THE WICKED SHALL PERISH, AND THE ENEMIES OF
THE LORD SHALL BE AS THE FAT OF LAMBS: THEY SHALL
CONSUME; INTO SMOKE SHALL THEY CONSUME AWAY.

21 THE WICKED BORROWETH, AND PAYETH NOT AGAIN:
BUT THE RIGHTEOUS SHEWETH MERCY, AND GIVETH.

22 FOR SUCH AS BE BLESSED OF HIM SHALL INHERIT THE
EARTH; AND THEY THAT BE CURSED OF HIM SHALL BE CUT
OFF.

23 THE STEPS OF A GOOD MAN ARE ORDERED BY THE
LORD: AND HE DELIGHTETH IN HIS WAY.

24 THOUGH HE FALL, HE SHALL NOT BE UTTERLY CAST
DOWN: FOR THE LORD UPHOLDETH HIM WITH HIS HAND.

25 I HAVE BEEN YOUNG, AND NOW AM OLD; YET HAVE I
NOT SEEN THE RIGHTEOUS FORSAKEN, NOR HIS SEED BEG-
GING BREAD.

26 HE IS EVER MERCIFUL, AND LENDETH; AND HIS SEED IS BLESSED.

27 DEPART FROM EVIL, AND DO GOOD; AND DWELL FOR EVERMORE.

28 FOR THE LORD LOVETH JUDGMENT, AND FORSAKETH NOT HIS SAINTS; THEY ARE PRESERVED FOR EVER: BUT THE SEED OF THE WICKED SHALL BE CUT OFF.

29 THE RIGHTEOUS SHALL INHERIT THE LAND, AND DWELL THEREIN FOR EVER.

30 THE MOUTH OF THE RIGHTEOUS SPEAKETH WISDOM, AND HIS TONGUE TALKETH OF JUDGMENT.

31 THE LAW OF HIS GOD IS IN HIS HEART; NONE OF HIS STEPS SHALL SLIDE.

32 THE WICKED WATCHETH THE RIGHTEOUS, AND SEEKETH TO SLAY HIM.

33 THE LORD WILL NOT LEAVE HIM IN HIS HAND, NOR CONDEMN HIM WHEN HE IS JUDGED.

34 WAIT ON THE LORD, AND KEEP HIS WAY, AND HE SHALL EXALT THEE TO INHERIT THE LAND: WHEN THE WICKED ARE CUT OFF, THOU SHALT SEE IT.

35 I HAVE SEEN THE WICKED IN GREAT POWER, AND SPREADING HIMSELF LIKE A GREEN BAY TREE.

36 YET HE PASSED AWAY, AND, LO, HE WAS NOT: YEA, I SOUGHT HIM, BUT HE COULD NOT BE FOUND.

37 MARK THE PERFECT MAN, AND BEHOLD THE UPRIGHT: FOR THE END OF THAT MAN IS PEACE.

38 BUT THE TRANSGRESSORS SHALL BE DESTROYED TOGETHER: THE END OF THE WICKED SHALL BE CUT OFF.

39 But the salvation of the righteous is of the Lord: he is their strength in the time of trouble.

40 And the Lord shall help them, and deliver them: he shall deliver them from the wicked, and save them, because they trust in him.

Once you have made the prayers over the glass of water with the camphor and evil eye beads in it, you want to set it by your front door somewhere. The ward is now ready to protect your house from the evil eye slipping its way in. As the eye is fixed on you so shall it be drowned in the waters and die.

It would be wise for you to actually make two of them—one for the front door and the other for the back door. Again, you can never have too much protection up and working for you. The ward needs to be refreshed about every two weeks. You refresh the ward by washing the beads, giving it more water, and replacing the camphor as needed. The beads need to be cleaned so they can remain on point when it comes to keeping your house protected.

UNCROSSING OIL

Along with cleansing and protection, uncrossing should be a constant that is always happening around you. Some folks look at uncrossing and cleansing as the same thing, however they are not exactly the same. They would be considered cousins. Whereas cleansing is meant to clean the spiritual mud off of you and remove things that have attached themselves to you, uncrossing is work that is done to stop tricks that may have been laid on you, work done against you, or things you have inadvertently done yourself that create obstacles. Uncrossing involves getting rid of those things, just as sometimes folks need to change their luck or open up the crossroads.

Ingredients:

- 1 white candle that can burn for three days, plus 14 white emergency candles

- 1 glass of water

- A plate

- 2 pints olive oil—to act as a carrier and bring a spirit of peace and new beginnings

- 1 whole Low John root—to remove work done against you and protect against work that may be done in the future

- 2 tablespoons agrimony—to cleanse and turn work away from you

- 2 tablespoons rue—to cleanse and protect; also has the ability to open roads and smooth the path you are walking

- 2 tablespoons peppermint (*Mentha piperita*)—to renew and refresh

- 2 tablespoons pine bark—to cleanse and provide protection that can weather many storms

- 1 quart-size Mason jar

Making the oil takes about three days of initial work and another fourteen days of prayers.

Take the roots and the oil to your work space. Place the roots on a plate.

Light your candle and have a glass of water nearby.

Orient the roots in all four directions to send the work to the four corners of the earth.

Once that is done, you are going to give some rum or whiskey and smoke to the roots.

Now you are going to begin to make your prayers and petitions over the roots. When you are making the prayers and petitions it is important that you are being specific about the job you want the roots to do. Think of yourself as the general of an army—you have to tell your soldiers what they need to do. Tell them that their job is to work uncrossing and to keep work off of you. Tell the roots to turn tricks away from you and send them back to where they came from. Speak to the spirits of the roots just as you would speak to your own spirits. This is important because the working relationship between you and the roots is what establishes potency in your work. Psalm 8 is a very good prayer to pray over this work, along with your own petitions. The power of breaking work done and trampling it under your feet is exactly what the root doctor calls for to make sure not a damn thing is going to cross you up. Psalm 8:

8 O Lord, our Lord, how excellent is thy name in all the earth! who hast set thy glory above the heavens.

2 Out of the mouth of babes and sucklings hast thou ordained strength because of thine enemies, that thou mightest still the enemy and the avenger.

3 When I consider thy heavens, the work of thy fingers, the moon and the stars, which thou hast ordained;

4 WHAT IS MAN, THAT THOU ART MINDFUL OF HIM? AND THE SON OF MAN, THAT THOU VISITEST HIM?

5 FOR THOU HAST MADE HIM A LITTLE LOWER THAN THE ANGELS, AND HAST CROWNED HIM WITH GLORY AND HONOUR.

6 THOU MADEST HIM TO HAVE DOMINION OVER THE WORKS OF THY HANDS; THOU HAST PUT ALL THINGS UNDER HIS FEET:

7 ALL SHEEP AND OXEN, YEA, AND THE BEASTS OF THE FIELD;

8 THE FOWL OF THE AIR, AND THE FISH OF THE SEA, AND WHATSOEVER PASSETH THROUGH THE PATHS OF THE SEAS.

9 O LORD OUR LORD, HOW EXCELLENT IS THY NAME IN ALL THE EARTH!

Pray this prayer seven times over the roots. The seven times is to complete a cycle and initiate a new beginning.

So, once you have made the prayers over the roots for that day, leave them in the workspace with the candle going. You are going to repeat this process for three days. Each day, you are going to make your prayers and petitions over the roots and continue to focus the work on what needs to be happening to be victorious in this uncrossing.

On the third day, you are going to make your prayers and petitions over the roots then put them into the Mason jar with the oil.

Take the jar in your hand and begin to shake it. When you are shaking it up, give those petitions over it and let it merge together. Let the roots that were once separate now become unified to work the magic that will uncross you and keep you uncrossed.

You will continue to have a candle lit, make your prayers and petitions over the oil, and shake the jar for the remaining fourteen days.

When the process is finished, you will have a potent defender against work done that will also aid in keeping your roads smooth because you won't have to deal with what folks throw at you and whether or not it sticks.

To use the oil, take a few drops and put it in your non-dominant palm. When you have the drops in your palm, you are going to begin to rub the oil toward yourself to draw the uncrossing work into yourself. That way, anything that is there can be dealt with and sent off of you. Some workers would have you rub it away from you but I don't agree. See, the nature of uncrossing work is indeed to take work off of you, but at the same time the work of uncrossing, or continual work of uncrossing, is that it makes a border of protection around you so it needs to be drawn into you first so it can handle what may already be there.

If you would like to, you can also use some of the oil in a bath. You can add it to a cleansing bath for additional power, but that is up to you. At the end of the day, if you are crossed up then you will always miss the mark. I say the hell with that. If I am going to live my life and do the work that I do, then you can trust and believe that I am not going to miss the mark. The same should apply to you. Be strong, be victorious, and never allow yourself to remain crossed up. If you do, you will always be trying to walk uphill without getting very far.

Never forget that inside of you is a powerful spirit, but sometimes the foolishness of others comes around to stop that spirit from soaring. This is one way to stop that foolishness dead in its tracks and show just how strong you really are.

SEPARATION POWDER

The work of separation is one of those things that folks can look at as being either positive or negative. For example, if you are trying to break up a marriage because you have a spouse that beats you, is verbally or mentally abusive, and the like, folks might say, "That's not a bad thing." If you are trying to separate a boss from an employee who is trying to manipulate them, that may not be a bad thing either. Then, there are the folks that want to break up a relationship because they want one of the halves of it. Well, it can certainly be done, however, the reasoning and perceived justification behind it is on you. I will tell you how to do it, but what you decide to do with it is between you and your own spirits.

ooooo

Ingredients:

- 1 candle (black or purple works well for this)
- 3 tablespoons of asafetida (*Ferula assa-foetida*)—to help drive a lack of desire to be around the individual with its horrible scent
- 3 tablespoons of cayenne pepper (*Capsicum annuum*)—to heat up work and make it strong, hot, and fast
- 3 tablespoons of Solomon's seal root—to bring command and control
- 3 tablespoons of dirt from the grave of someone who died with a broken heart

- 3 tablespoons of guinea pepper—to heat the work and sharpen it to cut effectively

- 3 tablespoons of sulphur—to send things away; just be careful because sulphur also can draw certain malevolent spirits (which isn't always a bad thing because they may aid in the work)

- 1 small wasp nest—to add a "sting" and a spirit of control to the work, also for moving away (separation), and adding an attitude of domination

- Some rum or whiskey

- A cigar or cigarette

- Mortar and pestle

- A container or bag to hold the roots

- A trowel

- A few coins

To fix a candle (optional):

- A black or purple candle

- A small amount of vegetable oil

- A photo or other personal item of the person you are doing the work on

Getting the dirt from the grave of someone who died with a broken heart can be a little tricky. First, you might have to do a little bit of research to find that particular grave. You can look up some of the folks in the graveyard on the Internet and see what you find. You can also simply talk to some older people who may have stories about folks in the graveyard that are indicative of what you are looking for. There is a reason why we talk to our elders. They have stories that are packed with information that can help add to your own growth. The spirit you are looking for can be someone who was divorced and had strong depression issues, someone who passed because they did not have a will to live, or someone who passed due to suicide as a result of a separation in relationship.

When you find that person, you will need to petition them for their help. You can find all of the instructions in chapter 9, Conjure in the Graveyard (page 89).

Now that you have all the ingredients, you are going to light the candle, get a glass of water, then take the ingredients and begin your offerings—rum or whiskey and smoke for each of the roots that are about to do a job of separation.

Once you have given the offerings to the roots and nest and oriented them to the four directions, you are going to begin to make your prayers and petitions over them. This is where you begin to speak words of separation over the roots, telling them that the job is to move apart two (or more) people. This is not the time to be timid or shy, but rather where you begin to command and speak as you would to an army about to go into a battle.

A good prayer to pray here comes from Exodus 8: "And I will put a division between my people and thy people: to morrow shall this sign be . . ."

Once the prayers and petitions are made, keep the roots with the light set on them. You need to repeat this part of the process for three days. Each day you are going to continue to make those petitions, declarations, and prayers over the roots.

After the third day is done, you are going to take the roots, which were separate, and bring them together. Here is where they begin to become unified in a single goal. In this case, the goal is separation, to drive a wedge. Once you have combined them together, you are going to get a mortar and pestle and begin to crush and beat them into a powder.

What is important about this part of it is while you are grinding and pounding, you are continuing to make those declarations and commands. The petitions need to be constant, as it adds to the potency of the work. Remember, you get out what you put in, so if you half-ass the job you get a half-ass result.

Once the roots have been pounded into dust, you are going to put it into a container, like a bag or something along those lines. Then, it is time for a little field trip. You are going to take the powder to a jail, or the grounds of a jail. There you are going to dig a little hole, put some coins and some rum or whiskey in it, and bury the powder there.

Why the jail? The jail is a place of separation. The dirt in the soil of the jail is one that holds with it all of the feelings and acts of keeping things apart. This is where the burying of the powder brings extra power to it and soaks it in the spirit of separation. The powder needs to be buried there for seven days. After the seventh day, you can go and dig it up. You must also give the ground offerings when you dig up the powder, so do not forget that part.

You may ask, "Why not just put the jail dirt in the powder?" In this case, we want to the powder to be bathed in it, not exactly a part of it. The reason for this is because we already have the dirt of the spirit in the graveyard and, unless you are looking for significant separation (e.g., them getting arrested) then it is not necessary. The essence of the dirt is enough to get the job done. You do not want it to overpower the rest of the work. Also, the spirit of the person who died with a broken heart is there to aid in the work.

Now, to use the powder, you have to be sneaky. The powder is something that the separation candidate needs to step in, sit in, or touch in some way. That is how the work begins. So, you can sprinkle it on the doorstep of the person or put it under his desk at work. You can also take some hairspray and spray his car door handle with it and sprinkle the powder on it. The hairspray will cause the powder to stick to it, you see, so they will touch it.

After that is done, you can fix a black or purple candle with the powder and some of the hair or a photo of the person or people involved. What you are going to do is take the candle and rub it with a little oil. Vegetable oil is fine. Then you are going to take the photo or hair and put it onto the candle. If you are using a photo, burn the photo into ash and sprinkle it onto the candle. Then you can sprinkle the powder onto the candle.

Light the candle and continue to speak the declarations, petitions, and prayers over it. Do *not* get the powder on your hands. You don't want to be the one going through the issues of separation. Unless, of course, you do want to be the person going through the separation.

If you accidentally get some of the powder on you, a cleansing is immediately needed. You should get some Florida Water, a couple pinches of salt, and a tablespoon of hyssop or rue and wash the area the powder touched. Put the ingredients together and scrub the area to get it off of you. Scrub for a couple of minutes and then you can wash the area with soap and water. See, these things know one thing and that is the job they do. If you touch it, the roots are going to do the job on you! So, you want to be careful. It's the same principle of someone who deals with fire. Sure, they can manipulate the fire, but at the end of the day the fire will always burn and will burn you if you aren't careful with it.

Again, these works are not about good or evil, moral or immoral, they are about balance. Balance is how we see things as rootworkers and it is that same balance that must be maintained. That is how we focus and how we work.

CROSSING POWDER

Crossing powder is one of my favorite tricks to lay. Yes, I do have favorites on both sides of the coin. Crossing powder is used to take someone's luck away, to *cross* them up, to shut down the roads, and to bring about blockages one after another. When we use the term "crossed up," we are talking about a condition where the roads and opportunities are shut down and where the luck of the individual goes out the window.

Ingredients:

- A black or red candle, plus another red or black candle

- A glass of water

- Some rum or whiskey

- A cigar or cigarette for smoke

- A nice big handful of pine needles (preferably dead)—to bring about the feeling of being uncomfortable and not knowing peace

- A few tablespoons of crossroads dirt from the X part of the crossroads—to shut down the roads; what I mean by the X part of the crossroads is the in-between part—if you are standing at an intersection, looking at the crossroads, you will see how the intersection makes a cross symbol. If you were to look at the in-between parts of that cross you will see how it makes an X—that is the part of the crossroads where you need to gather the dirt

- 2 tablespoons of guinea pepper—to heat the work as well as sharpen the trick so it hits hard and fast

- 2 tablespoons of wormwood (*Artemisia absinthium*)—to affect the mind

- Some dirt from the grave of someone who died a violent death

- Mortar and pestle

To fix a candle (optional):

- Personal items or photos of person you are working to cross

- A plate

- A small paper bag

- A few coins or other offerings

For the dirt from the grave of someone who died a violent death, again, you may have to do a little research to find someone, but it must be done. These spirits of people who died violent deaths are usually more than willing to do work that involves vengeance or justice because they didn't have it when they were alive, but some will help and some will not. When you find that person, you will need to petition them for their help (see page 89).

Once you have all the ingredients together, begin with the offerings—rum or whiskey and smoke for each of the roots that are about to do a job of crossing up someone's life. Have a glass of water and a black or red candle going. They are good for this kind of work.

When the offerings are made and the roots have been oriented to the four directions, you begin your prayers, petitions, and declarations over the roots. These prayers and declarations should be made in such a way that you are essentially commanding that the folks who come in contact with the powder will be crossed up, their roads will be closed, and their luck will have run out. Speak those declarations to the roots. Give them their jobs and when you do they will answer.

Just for clarity's sake, when I say "roots" I am referring to the dirts as well. They all are under the same umbrella to me. Now, just as with the separation powder, you are going to continue this process for three days. After the third day you will bring them together.

Just as before, with the mortar and pestle, you will pound and grind the ingredients down into a powder, all the while continuing to make those declarations of crossing up those who come in contact with it.

Once the powder is complete, you can add some talc as a carrier, if you like. That is, of course, up to you.

To work the powder, the same principle applies here as in the separation powder. The person needs to come in contact with it. As I explained before, there are several ways you can do that. How you do it is up to you.

Now, can you fix a candle with crossing powder to work someone in that way? Yes, you can. However, the effect may vary because direct contact holds the most potency. If you were to fix a candle you would need the link to the person to go into the candle. Again, it can be some hair, nails, photo, piece of unwashed clothing (burned into ash and rubbed into the candle), or something that has a direct link to them.

You would fix the candle in the same manner as you did the separation candle. The only additional thing you will do is to make a line of the crossing powder wherever you are going to set the candle. You take the powder and make an X, set the candle on top of it, and then light it up.

Once the candle is lit, you are going to call by name the person you are working and make those declarations over the candle, asking and commanding that their life be crossed, that their luck fall by the wayside, and that their roads be shut down.

Once the candle is done, you are going to take whatever wax is left over and put it in a little paper bag. Take it to the crossroads and bury it in the X part of the crossroads. Always make sure that when you bury something, you put an offering in the ground. Remember, we give something we take something, if we take something we give something.

If you were to decide to work the candle, I would work it in a cycle of seven or nine days. Those numbers are completions of cycles of work. It would be starting something and seeing it through to completion.

THE ROTTING TONGUE

The work of the rotting tongue is one that is meant to shut the mouth of your enemy. It can also be worked to bring harm. Yes, in this work harm is a part of it. A lot of folks like to shy away from that side of the coin, but it has its place just like blessing, healing, and other work. I remember the first time I gave a class on it, folks were squirming in their seats! The funny part was that everyone wanted to hear about it and learn. Just goes to show that there are always parts of us that want to know the other side of the coin, even if we don't admit it.

ooooo

Ingredients:

- A candle
- A glass of water

- A beef tongue (purchase from a butcher or supermarket)—to stand in for the tongue of person you want to silence

- 7 habanero peppers (*Capsicum chinense Habanero*)—to heat the work and cause discomfort

- A photograph or other personal item of the person you intend to do the work against (the photograph should show the target's entire face and ideally their hands)

- 1 regular new, unused sewing needle, plus one good-sized new, unused sewing needle

- A spool of black thread

- A bit of Spanish moss—to bind and stop individuals in their tracks; any redbugs in it add intensity

- 1 tablespoon of sulphur—to clear out bad spirits and attract worse ones

- 1 tablespoon of alum—to pucker the mouth to shut people up

- A little bit of gasoline

- Something to cover your head

- A few coins

- A cigar or cigarette for smoke

- A hammer

- 3 iron nails

- Some rum or whiskey

First, make sure you have a candle lit and a glass of water present.

To begin the work, slice the beef tongue down the side, making a pocket. The side, meaning the long part, horizontally down the tongue.

Cut the habanero peppers in half. You may want to wear gloves during this part. If you have ever touched your face, eyes, or other sensitive areas after handling hot peppers you will know exactly what I mean. It is not a pleasant experience.

Once the peppers are cut in half, you are going to remove and reserve the seeds. Take the pepper halves and begin to rub the tongue, inside the pocket, while focusing on the individual who is the target. Begin to speak the declarations over the work. Tell the work what it is supposed to do. This is the time for your emotions to come into play and for you to make the commands over the work.

When you have finished rubbing down the tongue, put a couple of the pepper halves inside the pocket, along with the seeds you have reserved.

Get the photograph and other personal items. Using the needle and black thread, sew the eyes and mouth on the photograph shut. If it shows her hands, then sew her hands together as well. The way you tie the hands together is to sew one hand closed then stitch over to the other hand. It should look as if both hands are bound together. Tie them up real good because this is part of how the work works.

Put the photograph in the pocket of the beef tongue. Place a bit of the Spanish moss in the pocket as well, on top of the photograph. Now add about a tablespoon of sulphur and a tablespoon of alum.

Once all the ingredients are inside the pocket of the tongue, you are going to take the good-size needle and that black thread and sew the pocket closed. When the pocket is sewn shut, take a little bit of gasoline and set it on fire. Run the tongue through the gasoline and heat it up. This kind of work you want to be hot, fast, and pointed.

Now it is time to take a little trip. Go to the graveyard at night or as close to it as possible. Be sure to cover your head for protection and bring your offerings to leave at the gate.

When you are inside the graveyard, you need to find the oldest tree there. This will be the place where you are going to set your work.

When you have found the tree, you are going to take the tongue out of the bag or whatever you put it in to bring it to the graveyard. Now, it is time to pray over it again. The absolute prayer and petition comes from Isaiah. I love this prayer for this work, specifically, because it is very much to the point. The prayer is Isaiah 54:

54 Sing, O barren, thou that didst not bear; break forth into singing, and cry aloud, thou that didst not travail with child: for more are the children of the desolate than the children of the married wife, saith the Lord.

2 Enlarge the place of thy tent, and let them stretch forth the curtains of thine habitations: spare not, lengthen thy cords, and strengthen thy stakes;

3 For thou shalt break forth on the right hand and on the left; and thy seed shall inherit the Gentiles, and make the desolate cities to be inhabited.

4 Fear not; for thou shalt not be ashamed: neither be thou confounded; for thou shalt not be put to shame: for thou shalt forget the shame of

THY YOUTH, AND SHALT NOT REMEMBER THE REPROACH OF THY WIDOWHOOD ANY MORE.

5 FOR THY MAKER IS THINE HUSBAND; THE LORD OF HOSTS IS HIS NAME; AND THY REDEEMER THE HOLY ONE OF ISRAEL; THE GOD OF THE WHOLE EARTH SHALL HE BE CALLED.

6 FOR THE LORD HATH CALLED THEE AS A WOMAN FOR-SAKEN AND GRIEVED IN SPIRIT, AND A WIFE OF YOUTH, WHEN THOU WAST REFUSED, SAITH THY GOD.

7 FOR A SMALL MOMENT HAVE I FORSAKEN THEE; BUT WITH GREAT MERCIES WILL I GATHER THEE.

8 IN A LITTLE WRATH I HID MY FACE FROM THEE FOR A MOMENT; BUT WITH EVERLASTING KINDNESS WILL I HAVE MERCY ON THEE, SAITH THE LORD THY REDEEMER.

9 FOR THIS IS AS THE WATERS OF NOAH UNTO ME: FOR AS I HAVE SWORN THAT THE WATERS OF NOAH SHOULD NO MORE GO OVER THE EARTH; SO HAVE I SWORN THAT I WOULD NOT BE WROTH WITH THEE, NOR REBUKE THEE.

10 FOR THE MOUNTAINS SHALL DEPART, AND THE HILLS BE REMOVED; BUT MY KINDNESS SHALL NOT DEPART FROM THEE, NEITHER SHALL THE COVENANT OF MY PEACE BE REMOVED, SAITH THE LORD THAT HATH MERCY ON THEE.

11 O THOU AFFLICTED, TOSSED WITH TEMPEST, AND NOT COMFORTED, BEHOLD, I WILL LAY THY STONES WITH FAIR COLOURS, AND LAY THY FOUNDATIONS WITH SAPPHIRES.

12 AND I WILL MAKE THY WINDOWS OF AGATES, AND THY GATES OF CARBUNCLES, AND ALL THY BORDERS OF PLEASANT STONES.

13 AND ALL THY CHILDREN SHALL BE TAUGHT OF THE LORD; AND GREAT SHALL BE THE PEACE OF THY CHILDREN.

14 IN RIGHTEOUSNESS SHALT THOU BE ESTABLISHED: THOU SHALT BE FAR FROM OPPRESSION; FOR THOU SHALT NOT FEAR: AND FROM TERROR; FOR IT SHALL NOT COME NEAR THEE.

15 BEHOLD, THEY SHALL SURELY GATHER TOGETHER, BUT NOT BY ME: WHOSOEVER SHALL GATHER TOGETHER AGAINST THEE SHALL FALL FOR THY SAKE.

16 BEHOLD, I HAVE CREATED THE SMITH THAT BLOWETH THE COALS IN THE FIRE, AND THAT BRINGETH FORTH AN INSTRUMENT FOR HIS WORK; AND I HAVE CREATED THE WASTER TO DESTROY.

17 NO WEAPON THAT IS FORMED AGAINST THEE SHALL PROSPER; AND EVERY TONGUE THAT SHALL RISE AGAINST THEE IN JUDGMENT THOU SHALT CONDEMN. THIS IS THE HERITAGE OF THE SERVANTS OF THE LORD, AND THEIR RIGHTEOUSNESS IS OF ME, SAITH THE LORD.

Pray this prayer three times over the tongue and name the person who is inside it. It is important that they be named because the direction of the work comes from both the link to the tongue and the declaration of the worker who is doing it.

Once the prayers and declarations have been made, you need to give offerings to the work. Blow some smoke on it and give it a little rum or whiskey. You also need to pour out a bit of rum or whiskey to the tree that you are going to set it in.

When that is done, you are going to get out the hammer and nails and nail the tongue to the tree. As you are driving the nails through the tongue and into the tree, speak to the work—that the individual will cease to talk, that should the individual find your name in their mouth, they will experience pain and rot, that every time your name comes out of their mouth, it is puckered and falls on deaf ears, or other words of that nature. This is the time for you to make sure you are clear with the work and how it is going to affect the target.

The tongue should not be set in a conspicuous place on the tree. You don't want other folks messing with your work. Hide the work the best you can and let it do its job. When you are finished there, walk away from it and don't look back at it. The job is now up to the work to complete. Your portion is done.

As the tongue begins to rot, so does the individual you are working against. Her actions against you can cause physical pain. This is a work that gains potency as the rot sets in. See, as everything mixes together and melds with the flesh of the tongue, so then does the work fuse to the job get done.

It is important that, after you finish doing the work, you take a cleansing bath. You don't want any unnecessary foolishness sticking to you. Sometimes we have to get our hands dirty and this is definitely one of those times. If you are going to work Conjure then you have to remember and respect both sides of that coin. That is and always has been the nature of this work.

DOMINATION BATH

This work of domination is one that is meant to draw influence over others and in some ways control them in order to achieve what you want to have happen. The other side of domination can be to bring you more self confidence so you can drive the boat, so to speak. This can be applicable to your love life, your work life, or just overall. One of the things with this bath is that it brings influence, but it also brings confidence to stand tall and to have your words adhered to. The goal of the bath is not only to bring your influence on others to the surface, but also to overcome any part of yourself that is lacking in the confidence to walk in domination of every situation.

For the bath, you are going to use what are called commanding roots. When we talk about commanding roots, we are talking about roots that have a spirit that brings the disposition to direct, dominate, or both. I like to tell folks that commanding roots could be compared to a general that oversees an army. They give direction, have the ability to bring a plan of action to fruition, and take a group that may be separate and bring unification in the job that needs to be done.

ooooo

Ingredients:

- 1 white candle, plus 1 red candle

- A glass of water

- 2 large pinches of licorice root (*Glycyrrhiza glabra*)—potent in works of domination and often used in works of domination in love or lust

- 2 large pinches of orris root (*Iris pallida*)—holds a spirit of influence that tends to draw folks to you with open ears; it works particularly well over a man

- 1 large pinch of Master of the Woods (*Asperula odorata*)—works well for conquering situations and overcoming circumstances and to turn the tides in your favor

- 1 large pinch of Solomon's seal root—has a strong element of control, particularly over the spirit nature

- 1 large pinch of lemon verbena (*Aloysia citrodora*)—wonderful for moving old things out and clearing the road for new things; it also has a spirit that brings luck and an upper hand in situations

- 1 medium-size pot

- Enough water to fill the pot

- 1 red candle—associated with passion, fire, and busting through obstacles to create a change

Now, take those roots and set them on a plate. Then get the white candle and a glass of water. Light the candle and present it and the roots to the four directions.

Next, you're going to begin to pray over them. For this, a great prayer to begin with is found in Isaiah 41:10–20:

10 FEAR THOU NOT; FOR I AM WITH THEE: BE NOT DIS-MAYED; FOR I AM THY GOD: I WILL STRENGTHEN THEE; YEA, I WILL HELP THEE; YEA, I WILL UPHOLD THEE WITH THE RIGHT HAND OF MY RIGHTEOUSNESS.

11 BEHOLD, ALL THEY THAT WERE INCENSED AGAINST THEE SHALL BE ASHAMED AND CONFOUNDED: THEY SHALL BE AS NOTHING; AND THEY THAT STRIVE WITH THEE SHALL PERISH.

12 THOU SHALT SEEK THEM, AND SHALT NOT FIND THEM, EVEN THEM THAT CONTENDED WITH THEE: THEY THAT WAR AGAINST THEE SHALL BE AS NOTHING, AND AS A THING OF NOUGHT.

13 FOR I THE LORD THY GOD WILL HOLD THY RIGHT HAND, SAYING UNTO THEE, FEAR NOT; I WILL HELP THEE.

14 FEAR NOT, THOU WORM JACOB, AND YE MEN OF ISRAEL; I WILL HELP THEE, SAITH THE LORD, AND THY REDEEMER, THE HOLY ONE OF ISRAEL.

15 BEHOLD, I WILL MAKE THEE A NEW SHARP THRESH-ING INSTRUMENT HAVING TEETH: THOU SHALT THRESH THE MOUNTAINS, AND BEAT THEM SMALL, AND SHALT MAKE THE HILLS AS CHAFF.

16 THOU SHALT FAN THEM, AND THE WIND SHALL CARRY THEM AWAY, AND THE WHIRLWIND SHALL SCAT-TER THEM: AND THOU SHALT REJOICE IN THE LORD, AND SHALT GLORY IN THE HOLY ONE OF ISRAEL.

17 WHEN THE POOR AND NEEDY SEEK WATER, AND THERE IS NONE, AND THEIR TONGUE FAILETH FOR THIRST, I THE LORD WILL HEAR THEM, I THE GOD OF ISRAEL WILL NOT FORSAKE THEM.

18 I WILL OPEN RIVERS IN HIGH PLACES, AND FOUNTAINS IN THE MIDST OF THE VALLEYS: I WILL MAKE THE WIL-DERNESS A POOL OF WATER, AND THE DRY LAND SPRINGS OF WATER.

19 I WILL PLANT IN THE WILDERNESS THE CEDAR, THE SHITTAH TREE, AND THE MYRTLE, AND THE OIL TREE; I WILL SET IN THE DESERT THE FIR TREE, AND THE PINE, AND THE BOX TREE TOGETHER:

20 THAT THEY MAY SEE, AND KNOW, AND CONSIDER, AND UNDERSTAND TOGETHER, THAT THE HAND OF THE LORD HATH DONE THIS, AND THE HOLY ONE OF ISRAEL HATH CREATED IT.

You can also make your own prayers over the roots, petition-ing for influence to be achieved and to dominate any and every situation. Here is one example:

I COME TO YOU, SPIRITS OF THE ROOTS AND ASK FOR YOUR HELP IN THIS JOB. I AM ASKING THAT YOU GIVE ME THE

ABILITY TO HOLD INFLUENCE OVER OTHERS AND TO DOM-
INATE EVERY SITUATION IN MY LIFE. I ASK THAT YOU GIVE
ME YOUR AID SO THAT WITH EVERY STEP I TAKE, CONFI-
DENCE AND INFLUENCE WILL POUR FROM ME. I ASK THAT
YOU COME TOGETHER AND GIVE ME THE ABILITY TO
BE THE ONE; THAT WHEN I TALK, PEOPLE WILL LISTEN.
GRANT ME THE POWER TO DRAW OTHERS TO ME AND GIVE
ME THE AUTHORITY TO MAKE THEM HEED MY WORDS. I
THANK YOU FOR WHO YOU ARE AND FOR WHAT YOU ARE
GOING TO DO TO ME. I GIVE YOU OFFERINGS OF WATER AND
LIGHT AS PAYMENT FOR THE WORK YOU ARE GOING TO DO
FOR ME. I HONOR YOU, WHO YOU ARE AND WHAT YOU WILL
DO. LET THIS WORK BE POTENT AND CHANGE THE CONDI-
TION THAT NEEDS TO BE REMEDIED. AMEN.

When you are praying, do not forget to name yourself and, if there are specific circumstances you are trying to dominate, name the condition as straightforwardly as possible. Do not forget that works of domination require confidence. If your confidence is not where it should be, then this bath can also be used to bring change to that condition so you will be more effective.

Once your prayers are made, take out the pot, fill it with water, and put it on the stove. Heat the water until it comes to a soft boil.

When it has reached the point of a soft boil, you can add the roots. When the roots have been added, let it cook for about ten to fifteen minutes. You should continue to make declarations over the roots while you are cooking them, such as, "I will dominate this situation," "I will be sure-footed in everything I do," "when I talk, people will listen," and so forth.

As it cooks, the water is going to turn brown, like the color of a tea. When it is finished cooking, take it off the stove and let it cool a bit.

While it is cooling, go to the bathroom and draw a bath. The bathwater needs to be very warm. You will also light that red candle in the bathroom.

When the ingredients in the pot have cooled enough so that you are able to take the bath, you can go ahead and bring it into the bathroom and pour it in the tub. After you have poured the bath into the tub, get into the water and sit for a minute. While you are sitting in the bath, you should be focusing on yourself and the work desired, in this case domination and influence. Begin to wash yourself from the feet upward to draw domination and influence into your life. While you are washing yourself, continue to make declarations as to what you want the work to do. You should be in the bath for at least ten to fifteen minutes so the roots and the work can soak in. Think of it like you are soaking in those spirits and their personalities and taking on those traits.

The best time for this bath is when the sun is setting. The time of transition of day to night is quite potent for changing conditions. This work is typically about making a change to circumstances around you, so just as the sun sets on what was going on with you, it sets on the old condition and the new condition begins—the new condition being that you are going to achieve the domination and influence you are looking for.

Usually, this bath takes more than one time to get results. Most of the time, when it comes to this specific work, I suggest it be done for seven days. This is to give time for the process of working in the spirit to manifest into the physical and for our minds to shift gears to receive the change that is needed. Seven days is also the completion of a cycle. The cycle opens the ability and opportunity that allow change to happen.

If you do the baths for seven days, you must be consistent and do them each day. If you begin a chain, it cannot be broken or the work will not be as effective. So, take the baths and wash domination and influence into your life so that your steps are sure-footed and your words hold the attention of whomever you meet!

HOT FOOT POWDER

To *hot foot* someone is to get them to leave, to abandon, and to move away from a place, physically. Just as the term indicates, the hot foot must move somewhere else so it can cool down, so to speak. Now, many people will ask, "Why?" Well, people have their own reasons for doing what they do. Perhaps they were wronged, perhaps the individual is a cause of constant unresolvable stress, or perhaps they are in a situation where they cannot leave and the other person refuses to. So, here we have the job of hot footing them to get them out.

Ingredients:

- A white candle

- A glass of water

- A Mason or other jar with a lid

- Either 7 red penny candles or 1 red seven-day candle

- Black pepper (*Piper nigrum*)—to heat up the work, bring an aggressive nature, and move people or situations away (the same goes for cayenne and hot peppers)

- Cayenne pepper

- Dried hot peppers, such as chilis

- Dirt from a post office, airport, bus station, or train station—to make someone travel away

- Some dried red ants—to irritate and keep the target from being able to sit still

- Mortar and pestle

Now, you might ask, "How am I going to get red ants?" The easy answer is to go to an ant pile and bring a Mason or bell jar with you as well as a trowel. Scoop right into the pile and put it in the jar quickly so they don't run everywhere. Then shut the lid and wait for them to die. If you don't have access to red ants where you are, you can always call a friend or someone who does and ask them to get them for you and send them to you.

Once you have all of the ingredients ready, you will take them all and put them on a plate, separately. Have the candle lit and the water present. You will now orient the plate of ingredients to the four directions (to send the work out) and then you will begin to make your prayers and declarations over it.

A great prayer for this work comes from Isaiah 59:1–8. It speaks of evildoings that have brought separation from God and have caused only crooked paths to be walked, never knowing peace, and their feet running to evil.

59 BEHOLD, THE LORD'S HAND IS NOT SHORTENED, THAT IT CANNOT SAVE; NEITHER HIS EAR HEAVY, THAT IT CANNOT HEAR:

2 BUT YOUR INIQUITIES HAVE SEPARATED BETWEEN YOU AND YOUR GOD, AND YOUR SINS HAVE HID HIS FACE FROM YOU, THAT HE WILL NOT HEAR.

3 FOR YOUR HANDS ARE DEFILED WITH BLOOD, AND YOUR
FINGERS WITH INIQUITY; YOUR LIPS HAVE SPOKEN LIES,
YOUR TONGUE HATH MUTTERED PERVERSENESS.

4 NONE CALLETH FOR JUSTICE, NOR ANY PLEADETH FOR
TRUTH: THEY TRUST IN VANITY, AND SPEAK LIES; THEY
CONCEIVE MISCHIEF, AND BRING FORTH INIQUITY.

5 THEY HATCH COCKATRICE' EGGS, AND WEAVE THE SPI-
DER'S WEB: HE THAT EATETH OF THEIR EGGS DIETH, AND
THAT WHICH IS CRUSHED BREAKETH OUT INTO A VIPER.

6 THEIR WEBS SHALL NOT BECOME GARMENTS, NEITHER
SHALL THEY COVER THEMSELVES WITH THEIR WORKS:
THEIR WORKS ARE WORKS OF INIQUITY, AND THE ACT OF
VIOLENCE IS IN THEIR HANDS.

7 THEIR FEET RUN TO EVIL, AND THEY MAKE HASTE
TO SHED INNOCENT BLOOD: THEIR THOUGHTS ARE
THOUGHTS OF INIQUITY; WASTING AND DESTRUCTION ARE
IN THEIR PATHS.

8 THE WAY OF PEACE THEY KNOW NOT; AND THERE IS
NO JUDGMENT IN THEIR GOINGS: THEY HAVE MADE THEM
CROOKED PATHS: WHOSOEVER GOETH THEREIN SHALL
NOT KNOW PEACE.

You can pray this prayer over the ingredients or you can use
one of your own. Also, if you are making the Hot Foot Powder for a specific individual, you should name them so the job
will be specifically directed toward them. As you are making
your prayers and declarations over the ingredients, remember
that you are going to focus on making the individuals who
come in contact with the powder leave—that they become
so uncomfortable where they are that they must get away as

quickly as possible. These are points you need to be declaring during this time.

When your prayers and declarations are finished, you will put the ingredients together and grind them—using a mortar and pestle, if you like. As the ingredients fuse together, they are coming to do a single job and hold a single purpose, which is to push someone away, physically.

Once everything has been ground down to a powder, place it in a jar. Cover the jar and set the powder somewhere that you can continue the work on it. The powder is not finished yet.

For each of the next seven days, you are going to light a red candle on the jar or next to the jar, depending on the candle. Once the candle is lit, you are going to make those prayers and declarations over the powder. If you are using penny candles on top of the jar, let them burn all the way down. Should you be using a seven-day candle (a tall candle encased in glass) next to the jar, let it burn for an hour each time. What is important is that you are consistent for that seven-day period of work so that it is effective. No skipping days! This work is better done at night, but can be done in the day as well.

After the seventh day, the powder is ready for use. As with Separation Powder and Crossing Powder, Hot Foot Powder is something that the intended individual needs to come in physical contact with to get the work started. See page 155 for suggestions.

It should also be noted that if you should spill the powder and accidentally step in it yourself, you should immediately take a cleansing bath because the powder does not differentiate between people (unless it's made for a specific person). You don't want to hot foot yourself!

EPILOGUE

The work of Conjure is something that was birthed out of the need to balance the scales, to overcome oppression, and be effective in the rebellion against the slave masters. It is for this reason that we work with both hands.

Conjure is something that I love and I have seen its results time and time again. I want to share with you a story about a client who came to me for work. For this purpose, her name will be called Faith.

One day, I was doing some work for another client. While I was doing this work, someone called me. I did not pick up the phone at the time because I was in the middle of working for the other client. When I finished, I looked at my phone and saw that I had a missed call. I called the number back and Faith answered the phone. She thanked me for calling her back and then proceeded to have a breakdown on the phone. She was crying, very upset, and felt hopeless.

I asked her what was going on and she explained that she had just gone to the doctor and had some tests done. The tests revealed that she had some sort of growth or lump in her breast. She explained to me that the doctors were quite concerned about it because of what it apparently looked like to them. They had spoken to her about the real and distinct possibility that she had breast cancer. The doctors said to her that they needed to biopsy the growth/lumps to know for sure, but they did not seem hopeful. She had to go and have the procedure done the following day.

Faith was telling me that she thought she might have cancer and she didn't know what she would do. She asked me if I could do anything to help her, that she was going to go have the tests done the next day. I spoke words of edification, hope, and strength to her and told her that I would do everything I could for her.

She continued to cry and was feeling horrible, but she allowed herself to calm down. I told her that we have spirits that are always by our side. Our ancestors, who paved the way for us, are the strength and foundation we stand on. They have the power to bring healing and restoration. Just as our other spirits hold authority, so do they. The power of the relationship we hold with our spirits can make or break us as individuals.

After she hung up the phone, I began to do work for her. I went to my ancestors and cried out to them to bring healing, to curse any cancer that may be there, and to restore what needed to be restored.

I fixed a lamp for Faith. The term *fixed* means that I put roots, oils, and such into it to get it to do a job. The job, in this case, was healing. Once the lamp was fixed, I began to make prayers and declarations over it for Faith. As I was doing that, my focus was on her healing and making my petitions heard. I felt my ancestors come and I could feel they were beginning to work on the situation. Then, I got a quickening in my spirit and heard "we hear you."

I heard back from Faith after the tests had been completed and the biopsy done. She was very, very happy to tell me that the tests came back that it was benign. Immediately, I thanked my spirits for their aid and working this wonderful thing for her.

As a servant of the spirit, you become the vessel they work through. We take the roots, the ancestors, and the strength of who we are to work Conjure and to work it effectively. I will not take credit for what they did in this situation, I only thank them for allowing me to be the vessel that facilitates magical change. In this case, a wonderful change!

When we work with the understanding that we are but the vessels of the spirit, it makes us more effective workers. This is because sometimes pride, ego, and a need to be noticed can get in the way of what the spirits and the ancestors are trying to accomplish.

When you grasp the nature of the ancestors, the nature of the spirit of the root, and the need for balance, it will enable you to be an effective worker in all that you do. The positive and negative sides are equally necessary because of the need this work was birthed from. It is my prayer that you gained some understanding into the work of Conjure and that you honor it as it should be honored. Respect, honor, and gratitude are fundamental to keeping this work going and to holding the integrity that encompasses it.

I would like to end this with a prayer for each and every one of you:

> I WANT TO THANK THE ANCESTORS FOR THEIR SACRIFICE, FOR PAVING THE WAY, FOR BLAZING THE TRAIL THAT YOU STAND ON RIGHT NOW. I GIVE THANKS FOR EVERYTHING THEY HAVE DONE FOR US AND EVERYTHING THEY ARE GOING TO DO. I GIVE THEM HONOR AND RESPECT AND PRAY THAT THEY GUIDE YOUR FEET TO WALK THE PATH

YOU ARE MEANT TO WALK. I PRAY THAT THE SPIRITS
OF THE ROOTS REVEAL THEMSELVES TO YOU AND THAT
THE RELATIONSHIP TO WORK WITH THEM BECOMES AS
STRONG AND DEEP AS THE TREE THAT IS PLANTED BY THE
WATER. I ASK THAT BLESSINGS ABOUND IN EACH OF YOUR
LIVES AND THAT THE POWER OF THIS WORK BECOMES AS
STRONG AS THE HEARTBEAT OF THE SPIRIT ITSELF. I ALSO
PRAY THAT AS YOU WALK IN THE CULTURE AND WORK
OF CONJURE, YOU GAIN THE STRENGTH TO OVERCOME
EVERY OBSTACLE, AND RECEIVE EVERY BLESSING COMING
YOUR WAY. BE BLESSED AND MAY THE AUTHORITY OF THE
CROSSROADS ALWAYS BE OPEN TO YOU.

GLOSSARY

balance—The necessity to keep things in order by doing spiritual work that is needed.

both hands—A term used in work that can define if it is positive or negative.

   right hand—Considered to be work of a positive nature.

      bless—To bring positive results and open doors for positive things to occur.

      heal—To change a condition of the body, the mind, or the spirit that removes adverse symptoms and makes whole what was broken.

      open—To create opportunity so that things run smoothly and conditions improve.

   left hand—Considered to be work of a negative nature.

      close—To shut down opportunity or stop things from happening.

      curse—Work of a negative nature that can inflict harm to the body, mind, and spirit.

hex—Work done to cross or close conditions and create problems for an individual.

justice—Work of balance that rights a wrong—this applies to both positive and negative work.

trick/lay a trick—A work done that brings bad luck, chaos, and problems and increases negative conditions.

vengeance—The work of giving a comeuppance for a wrong done.

change—To take a condition and shift it into another or to bring about a transition from one side to the other.

conduit—A means by which the spirit travels or moves through, something that holds the ability to open a spiritual door.

Conjure—Magic work that has a primary root in the Congo part of Africa and made its way to America by way of the slave trades.

culture—Spiritual work that is fused into day-to-day living—living your work, not simply doing spiritual work.

path—The place we walk in Conjure that brings edification to the ancestors as well as wisdom in our spiritual work; the trail that was blazed by the ancestors so we would have a foundation to stand on.

work—Spiritual labor that creates magical change to conditions or circumstances.

crossroads—The place of power where the world of the physical and the world of the spirit intersect; also the literal crossroads.

cycle, completion of a cycle—To begin a work and see it through to completion; a progression of spiritual work.

dirts—Soil of the earth that is gathered in specific places to do specific things. For example, money work being done would benefit from dirt from a bank because that dirt holds the essence of money.

doll baby—A doll that can be used to do spiritual work for or against individuals; there are many ways they can be made and many different types of work that can be done with a doll baby.

dollie—See *doll baby*.

domination—Work that is done to create influence and control over situations or people.

drawing—Work done that brings things to you, such as money, love, and healing.

dressing—To fix something, such as a candle, with oils and roots in preparation for spiritual work.

edification—To build up, give thanksgiving for, and elevate with prayers.

elevation—See *edification*.

evil eye—Spiritual work that is often birthed out of jealousy and envy and may be done subconsciously to cross someone up.

fixing (example, a candle or lamp)—See *dressing*.

Florida Water—A spiritual cologne used for cleansing and offerings.

foundation—Spiritual wisdom and strength that create a platform to stand on.

four directions—East, West, North, and South.

heating, heated—To bring assertiveness to spiritual work.

holy water—Water that has been blessed.

home training—Being raised like you have some sense; the process by which manners are attained.

light set—To to pray over a candle and light it in order to change a condition or open up a spiritual door.

magic—Divine power used to create change in conditions or circumstances.

make (as in prayers)—To pray, utter, or speak words to spirits and/or god that make petitions or bring edification; to declare a change in a condition.

mojo hand—A small bag or pouch that is made to do a spiritual work for an individual.

Nkisi—A carved wooden statue that houses a spirit.

offerings—Giving of items that a spirit will like.

personal items—Something belonging to an individual that carries their essence; also called *personal concerns* or *tokens*.

> **links**—Things such as hair, fingernails, blood, semen, skin.

> **name papers**—A paper with someone's name written on it used in spiritual work.

prayers—To pray, utter, or speak words to spirits and/or god that make petitions or bring edification; to declare a change in a condition.

- **declarations**—Statements made to create change in conditions.

- **petitions**—Utterances and requests made to the spirit to create magic change.

predisposition—The character one holds in their physical life as well as their spiritual life.

read on—To do a divination on a particular situation.

relationship—A closeness to your spirits, likened to that of a family.

reversal—To send a spiritual work or condition back to the originator.

roots—Plants, herbs, and items used in Conjure.

agrimony (*Agrimonia eupatoria*)—Used in cleansing work and some reversal work.

allspice (*Pimenta dioica*)—Used in prosperity and money-drawing work.

angelica root (*Angelica archangelica*)—Used in protection and cleansing work.

arrowroot powder (*Maranta arundinacea*)—Used to draw luck to you.

asafetida (*Ferula assa-foetida*)—Used in separation work.

bay (*Laurus nobilis*)—Used in shielding.

bayberry root (*Myrica pensylvanica*)—Used in money-drawing work.

black pepper (*Piper nigrum*)—Used to heat up work, to make work more assertive, and to move people or circumstances away.

calendula (*Calendula officinalis*)—Used in works of healing.

camphor (*Cinnamomum camphora*)—Used in works of cleansing and to stop the evil eye.

cayenne pepper (*Capsicum annuum*)—Used to heat work up and to give it an assertive nature.

cinnamon (*Cinnamomum spp*)—Used in works of domination, money, and to bring additional potency.

ginger root (*Zingiber officinale*)—Used in assertive work to draw things to you.

guinea pepper (*Aframomum melegueta*)—Used in works of domination, laying tricks, and to heat aggressive work.

habanero peppers (*Capsicum chinense Habanero*)—Used in aggressive works to bring discomfort.

High John the Conqueror root (*Convolvulus jalapa*)—Used to overcome obstacles and remove blockages; I also call the wrecking ball.

hyssop (*Hyssopus officinalis*)—Used in works of cleansing and healing of the body, spirit, and mind.

licorice root (*Glycyrrhiza glabra*)—Used in works of domination, lust, and, in some cases, for love.

Life Everlasting (*Helichrysum stoechas*)—Used in works of healing.

lime (*Citrus aurantifolia*)—Used in works of cleansing and to break work that may have been done against you; also used to break negativity.

Low John root (*Trillium pendulum*)—Used in work to remove negativity, keep evil away, and send back work done against you.

Master of the Woods (*Asperula odorata*)—Used in healing work and to strengthen any work that is being done; also used in works of conquering and overcoming.

orange (*Citrus reticulata*)—Used in work to draw money and prosperity.

orris root (*Iris pallida*)—Used in work where influence is needed; particularly effective with a man.

peppermint (*Mentha piperita*)—Used in uncrossing work and to bring renewal and refreshing of the spirit.

pine (*Pinus*)—Used in cleansing work; however, the dead needles of the pine can also be used in work to cross someone up.

rue (*Ruta graveolens*)—Used in work of cleansing and protection.

Solomon's seal root (*Polygonatum biflorum*)—Used in works of commanding and control; also used to focus the work at hand and to increase potency.

Spanish moss (*Tillandsia usneoides*)—Used in works of binding and slowing and in work of laying tricks.

thyme (*Thymus vulgaris*)—Used in prosperity work as well as drawing work.

wormwood (*Artemisia absinthium*)—Used in work to affect the mind.

commanding roots—Roots that command, act as a general in an army of spiritual work.

hot roots—Roots and herbs of an assertive nature.

rootworker—Someone who works in Conjure and specializes in the spiritual side of working the roots.

separation—Spiritual work that pulls things or individuals apart, away from one another.

service (to ancestors)—Spiritual work done to strengthen relationships with the ancestors by which offerings are given, prayers are made, and food is enjoyed.

spirits—Beings without bodies.

> **ancestors**—Spirits who come from your blood, primarily, who make it their mission for you to continue in your work and be successful at it.

> **dirts**—Spirits or essences that inhabit the dirt of specific places by which they hold a power to do work.

> **place**—Overall spirit or essence of a particular area.

> **roots**—The essence of a root that gives it a disposition toward doing specific kinds of work.

transition points—Points where there is a shift in both the physical and spiritual world that, in and of themselves, hold a power that can be utilized in spiritual work.

two mirrors—Representations of the physical and the spirit worlds, by which one is reflected back into the other.

> **physical realm**—The world of the mundane, the natural.

> **spirit realm**—The world of the spirit, the supernatural.

tying—Binding together, whether to seal or to render someone or something unable to continue.

ward—An item that does work in a home, business, or car to keep evil away.

work, works, worker—Spiritual labor that is done to manifest magical change in a condition, the life of someone, or in circumstances.

wrap—To bind.

away direction—Wrapping away from you is for sending out and for sending things far in the other direction.

toward direction—Wrapping toward you is to draw to you.

head—The crown, where the spirit can be seated.

ABOUT THE AUTHOR

 HOODOO SEN MOISE learned Conjure and Hoodoo as a child from his family. Now among the foremost authorities on the topic, he is also an initiated practitioner of several African Diaspora traditions. Hoodoo Sen Moise teaches throughout the US, as well as internationally. He resides in New Orleans, where he is co-owner of the shop Conjure New Orleans.

TO OUR READERS

Weiser Books, an imprint of Red Wheel/Weiser, publishes books across the entire spectrum of occult, esoteric, speculative, and New Age subjects. Our mission is to publish quality books that will make a difference in people's lives without advocating any one particular path or field of study. We value the integrity, originality, and depth of knowledge of our authors.

Our readers are our most important resource, and we appreciate your input, suggestions, and ideas about what you would like to see published.

Visit our website at *www.redwheelweiser.com* to learn about our upcoming books and free downloads, and be sure to go to *www.redwheelweiser.com/newsletter* to sign up for newsletters and exclusive offers.

You can also contact us at *info@rwwbooks.com* or at

Red Wheel/Weiser, LLC
65 Parker Street, Suite 7
Newburyport, MA 01950